STEVE JACKSON & IAN LIVINGSTONE

# BLOODBONES

## By Jonathan Green

## Illustrated by Tony Hough

Wizard Books

Published in the UK in 2010 by Wizard Books,
an imprint of Icon Books Ltd., Omnibus Business Centre
39–41 North Road, London N7 9DP
email: info@iconbooks.co.uk
www.iconbooks.co.uk/wizard

Previously published by Wizard Books in 2006

Sold in the UK, Europe, South Africa and Asia
by Faber & Faber Ltd., Bloomsbury House
74–77 Great Russell Street, London WC1B 3DA  or their agents

Distributed in the UK, Europe, South Africa and Asia
by TBS Ltd., TBS Distribution Centre, Colchester Road,
Frating Green, Colchester CO7 7DW

Published in Australia in 2010 by Allen & Unwin Pty. Ltd.,
PO Box 8500, 83 Alexander Street, Crows Nest, NSW 2065

Distributed in Canada by Penguin Books Canada,
90 Eglington Avenue East, Suite 700, Toronto,
Ontario M4P 2Y3

ISBN: 978-1-84831-119-0

Typesetting by Hands Fotoset, Mapperley, Nottingham

Printed and bound in the UK by
Clays of Bungay

FIGHTING FANTASY

## *Fighting Fantasy*: new Wizard editions

1. The Warlock of Firetop Mountain
2. The Citadel of Chaos
3. Deathtrap Dungeon
4. Stormslayer
5. Creature of Havoc
6. City of Thieves
7. Bloodbones
8. Night of the Necromancer

## Also available in the original Wizard editions

6. Crypt of the Sorcerer
7. House of Hell
8. Forest of Doom
9. Sorcery! 1: The Shamutanti Hills
10. Caverns of the Snow Witch
11. Sorcery! 2: Kharé – Cityport of Traps
12. Trial of Champions
13. Sorcery! 3: The Seven Serpents
14. Armies of Death
15. Sorcery! 4: The Crown of Kings
16. Return to Firetop Mountain
17. Island of the Lizard King
18. Appointment with F.E.A.R.
19. Temple of Terror
20. Legend of Zagor
21. Eye of the Dragon
22. Starship Traveller
23. Freeway Fighter
24. Talisman of Death
25. Sword of the Samurai
27. Curse of the Mummy
28. Spellbreaker
29. Howl of the Werewolf

**For Jake and Mattie**

**Avast me hearties!**

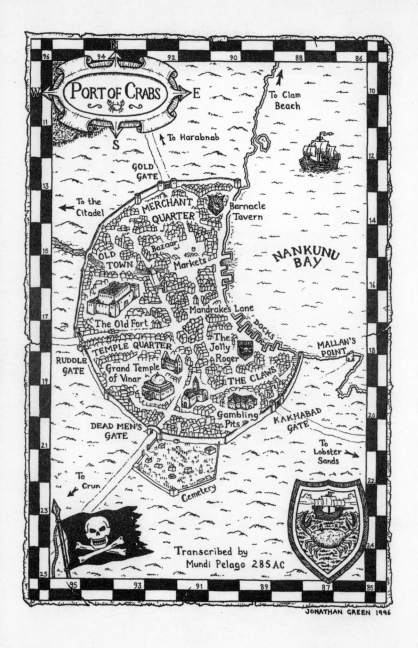

# CONTENTS

## HOW WILL YOU START
## YOUR ADVENTURE?

The book you hold in your hands is a gateway to another world – a world of dark magic, terrifying monsters, brooding castles, treacherous dungeons and untold danger, where a noble few defend against the myriad schemes of the forces of evil. Welcome to the world of **Fighting Fantasy**!

You are about to embark upon a thrilling fantasy adventure in which **YOU** are the hero! **YOU** decide which route to take, which dangers to risk and which creatures to fight. But be warned – it will also be **YOU** who has to live or die by the consequences of your actions.

Take heed, for success is by no means certain, and you may well fail in your mission on your first attempt. But have no fear, for with experience, skill and luck, each new attempt should bring you a step closer to your ultimate goal.

Prepare yourself, for when you turn the page you will enter an exciting, perilous **Fighting Fantasy** adventure where every choice is yours to make, an adventure in which **YOU ARE THE HERO**!

How would you like to begin your adventure?

**If you are new to Fighting Fantasy …**
You probably want to start playing straightaway. Just turn over to the next page and start reading. You may not get very far first time but you'll get the hang of how Fighting Fantasy gamebooks work.

**If you have played Fighting Fantasy before …**
You'll realise that to have any chance of success, you will need to discover your hero's attributes. You can create your own character by following the instructions on pages 219–225, or, to get going quickly, you may choose one of the existing Fighting Fantasy adventurers described on pages 216–218. Don't forget to enter your character's details on the Adventure Sheet which appears on pages 226–227.

**Game Rules**
It's a good idea to read through the rules which appear on pages 219–225 before you start. But as long as you have a character on your Adventure Sheet, you can get going without reading the Rules – just refer to them as you need to.

# BACKGROUND

It all started ten years ago when the evil pirate-lord Cinnabar murdered your family. At the time you were only twelve years old and lived with your family in the small fishing village of Clam Beach on the northern coast of Ruddlestone, half-way between the two major ports of the kingdom: Harabnab, home to all lawful adventurers and sailors, and the sinister Port of Crabs. Life in Clam Beach was not easy but it did have a peaceful security about it. And then the terrible day came.

It was a clear summer's day in Warming when the huge, forbidding, black galleon sailed into the bay, flying the dreaded flag of the skull and crossbones: pirates. The bloodthirsty cutthroats were soon racing up the beach towards the village. The fighting was swift and bloody. Soon most of the men folk of Clam Beach had been killed, your father and two brothers dying whilst trying to defend the village. In the end the village elders had no choice but to surrender to the marauding raiders and open the village's meagre treasure coffers. The cruel pirate captain came ashore from his ship to collect the booty himself. The sight of him filled you with awe and fear. The pirate was a tall, handsome man with a neatly trimmed, pointed black beard and his hair tied back in a ponytail. He was dressed in the clothes of a nobleman, with a fine scarlet coat, trimmed with gold braid, and wearing a large tricorn hat. At his waist hung a gleaming cutlass and you could not help noticing that on the back of his right hand was tattooed the image of a grinning, black skull. When the raiders had finally gone, filled with feelings of hatred for those who had murdered your family, you asked Raguy, the village soothsayer, who the pirate captain was. 'That villain is one of the most evil men ever to sail the twelve seas of Titan!' was his vehement reply. 'He is one of the most feared pirate-lords of our age, a creature without remorse, a murderer, and a follower of the bloodthirsty voodoo death-god Quezkari, whose mark is the black skull. His name is Cinnabar, but because of the terrible atrocities he commits he is also known as Bloodbones.' From that moment you vowed that, one day, you would have your revenge on the evil Cinnabar.

Your mother became ill soon after that dreadful day and three years later she died. On your sixteenth birthday you left Clam Beach and made your way to Harabnab, gaining the position of cabin boy on a ship travelling to the distant continent of Allansia. So it is that for the last six years you have sailed all across the globe, but you never forgot the promise you made to yourself a decade ago. Over many voyages you have tried to learn as much as you can about the rogue captain. You discovered that Cinnabar's galleon, the *Virago*, is frequently seen sailing in the waters around Nankunu Bay and that he has a hidden base somewhere close to the Port of Crabs. You also gleaned as much information as you could about the notorious city. And so, when you decided that you were at last ready to confront your enemy and the chance of passage on a merchant ship sailing to the Port of Crabs came up, you leapt at the opportunity. Vengeance, you are sure, will soon be yours.

The Port of Crabs is haven to every pirate, buccaneer and freebooter who ply their trade off the coast of the kingdom of Ruddlestone in the Old World. As you stand at the prow of the merchantman, looking towards the land, you can make out the ramshackle jumble of buildings of the infamous city and the outline of the Old Fort that stands above it like some ancient, crumbling sentinel. The merchantman bumps against the stone jetty and you quickly disembark. Not only is the Port of Crabs one of the most dangerous cities in the Old World, but a thick fog is starting to roll in from the sea. It is late afternoon on a chill day in Unlocking and the docks are bustling with activity. Standing close to the quayside is a large, old stone building, which looks like it could withstand a battering from Hydana, God of the Deep, himself. Hanging over its sturdy oak door is a faded sign declaring that this is the Jolly Roger. This seems as good a place as any to begin your search for Cinnabar, so you enter the inn.

The spacious bar inside the Jolly Roger is packed with all manner of scurvy-looking sailors and other low-lifes. The landlord is as big as an ox and has a large anchor tattooed on one arm. No one takes any notice of you as you enter, so you approach the bar and order a tankard of ale (deduct 1 Gold Piece from your

*Adventure Sheet*). You decide to question the landlord about Cinnabar first. Over your tankard of ale you talk about the weather and the state of trade and then draw the innkeeper onto the subject of the pirate you seek. 'I hear the *Virago* plies these waters,' you say. 'I'm surprised we weren't attacked ourselves.'

'Not anymore it doesn't,' the landlord replies. 'Have you not heard? Cinnabar has been dead these last six months.'

Cinnabar dead? You have come all this way, after years of harbouring desires for revenge, only to find that the dread pirate-lord has already passed from this world! You ask the landlord how he died. 'Have you not heard? I would've thought that everyone as far as the Diamond Islands would know by now. It all happened last Hiding.' You listen attentively as the innkeeper relates the tale. It appears that Cinnabar and his crew were emptying the hold of a galley sailing from Harabnab to Arkleton, in distant Analand, when the renowned bounty hunter Conyn caught up with them in his ship, the *Fortune*. Unable to escape, Cinnabar and his men had to defend themselves against the crews of the galley and Conyn. Fierce fighting ensued with Cinnabar eventually falling at Conyn's hand, having suffered an incredible number of wounds, his body being lost to the sea. With their leader killed, the surviving members of his crew fled aboard the *Virago*, returning to the Port of Crabs. Soon after, Cinnabar's second-in-command, Mirel the Red, set off in the *Virago* amid terrible storms, purportedly to recover her captain's body. 'Many now believe that the pirate-lord's galleon sank as it has not been seen since,' the landlord says, concluding his story. You thank him for his help and, in a bewildered daze, you make to leave the inn. You console yourself with the thought that at least the murderer of your family has at last been brought to justice.

As you leave the Jolly Roger you feel someone pulling on your jerkin. Turning round you discover that an old drunk, slumped at a table by himself, is the one trying to attract your attention. 'Just because he's dead doesn't mean he's at rest,' mutters the drunk. Curious about the drunk's words, you sit down opposite the old man and ask him what he means. 'Let's just say you don't want to go believing everything you hear. But I know what's going on. Oh yes, old Dregg knows. Cinnabar isn't *really* dead see, and he's coming back!' the old man says in a harsh whisper. Intrigued, you press Dregg to tell you more but he suddenly becomes serious and looks round the barroom uneasily. 'Not here. Meet me outside in ten minutes.' You nod in agreement and leave the Jolly Roger.

Tendrils of fog are now swirling around the boats in the harbour and oozing along the streets of the town. When the ten minutes are up you quickly return to the Jolly Roger and sneak down the side alley next to it. In the mist and shadows at the end of the narrow alleyway you can make out three figures standing over a fourth, cowering on the ground at their feet. Wasting no time, you draw your sword and dash towards them. Hearing your approach the three pirates turn to face you. The burly characters are ugly, scarred rogues and the biggest of them, who is easily wielding a heavy wooden club in one hand and holding a bullwhip in the other, looks as if he has some Ogre blood in his lineage. At the pirates' feet lies Dregg, beaten, bruised and only just conscious. 'Here's the snooper,' growls the Half-Ogre. 'You're no match for us. By the time we've finished with you, you'll be feeding the shrimps. Or rather the shrimps'll be feeding *on* you.' The other two pirates burst into coarse laughter at their companion's joke. 'Yeah, you're fishbait!'

Turn to paragraph 1.

**1**

Still laughing, the ruffians advance towards you. Apart from the Half-Ogre, there is a well-built bearded man, missing most of his teeth, and a leaner rogue with two ugly red scars running down the right-hand side of his face. Will you:

| | |
|---|---|
| Try to escape? | Turn to **135** |
| Charge one of the pirates? | Turn to **357** |
| Stand firm and prepare to fight the rogues? | Turn to **74** |

**2**

On your trek through the jungle you come upon two strange plants. One is a large bush with serrated-edged leaves and the other is a palm-like tree, the fronds of which are striped orange and black. The leaves of the Blade Bush are strong enough to be used as weapons so if you have lost your sword you may break off a Blade Leaf to use instead. The Tiger Palm is known to help in the healing of wounds. You may take some of the fronds which when applied to injuries after one battle will restore up to half the STAMINA points lost in that battle. Having taken what you want, turn to the paragraph with the number you noted down previously.

**3**

The Troll possesses nothing that might help you in your quest. Leaving the body lying in the filthy water, you set about trying to find a way out of this stinking hole. *Test your Luck*. If you are Lucky, turn to **171**. If you are Unlucky, turn to **193**.

## 4

After your encounter with the soul-chilling spirit you just want to leave the room as quickly as you can. Slamming the door to the cabin shut behind you, will you:

| | |
|---|---|
| Open the right-hand door? | Turn to **202** |
| Go down into the hold? | Turn to **26** |
| Leave the ship? | Turn to **72** |

## 5

Studying the *Arcanum*, it soon becomes apparent that it is Erasmus the Wizard's Book of Spells. You find several charms which you think you might be able to learn. However, you only have time to learn one from the following list.

*Fortune's Favour* – casting this spell restores up to 3 LUCK points.

*Trueskill* – once cast, the next time you have to *Test your Skill* you can avoid the roll and take it as if you were successful.

*Voodoo Vexer* – whenever you are attacked by Zombies, casting this spell will repel 1–3 of them (roll one dice and halve the result, rounding fractions down) so you do not have to fight them.

*Insect Repellent* – if ever you are bothered by insects, regardless of their size, this spell will keep them away from you so that you can avoid combat.

Each time you cast a spell you must reduce your STAMINA score by 2 points. Now will you:

Look at the *Mythica*?                    Turn to **47**
Examine the potions more closely?         Turn to **217**
Leave the cell?                           Turn to **385**

## 6

Taking flight, you hear a sharp crack behind you and then find yourself falling forwards as the Half-Ogre's whip wraps around your ankles and your feet are pulled from beneath you. Lose 2 STAMINA points. Dropping his whip, the Half-Ogre moves in to attack you with his club.

HALF-OGRE                    SKILL 8          STAMINA 9

If the Half-Ogre wins an Attack Round, roll one dice. On a roll of 6, the blow from his club knocks you off your feet. This means that you spend the next round of combat getting up again, so you must reduce your Attack Strength by 2 points for that Attack Round. If you kill the Half-Ogre, turn to **328**.

## 7

'You're too late,' gasps Ramatu with his dying breath. 'The ritual is complete; Cinnabar is invulnerable.' And then he is dead. You have rid the world of the evil Ramatu, Quezkari's servant – congratulations! Regain 1 LUCK point. There is no time to lose, Cinnabar must be on his way back to the Port of Crabs right now! As you prepare to leave the temple in pursuit of the Pirate-Lord you catch sight of the altar at the base of Quezkari's statue. On it is a fetish of the dark god-spirit and a sparkling, fist-sized pearl. Do you want to:

Pick up the fetish?            Turn to 210
Take the pearl?            Turn to 388
Leave the temple immediately?      Turn to 188

## 8

The ward you have chosen is in fact a Spirit Jewel, which has the power to drain the unearthly energies of denizens of the Ethereal Plane. When you finally confront Quezkari reduce his SKILL score by 3 points and his STAMINA by 6 and regain 1 LUCK point. Hissing in anger, the Arch-Spirit advances on you. Turn to 177.

## 9

Beneath a brightly painted banner, bearing his name, sits the Amazing Armarno. The man has the look of a Lendlelander about him, with sallow skin, slanting eyes and a long, thin moustache. He is performing a trick with three playing cards and has attracted a small crowd of curious onlookers. Two of the cards are black, one is white, and the aim of the game seems to be to guess which of the cards is the white one when they have been shuffled and laid face down on the small table in front of the man. To play the game you have to place a stake of 2 Gold Pieces to win a potential prize of 10 Gold Pieces, although at the moment no one seems to be having much luck against Armarno. If you want to play, turn to 32: if not you can either move on to the Arrow of Providence (turn to 81) or Calabrius's Calculator (turn to 294), or leave the Gambling Pits altogether (turn to 207).

## 10

Coming to the edge of an escarpment you find yourself looking out over the sparkling waters of a large lagoon, linked to the sea by a narrow channel on the far side. And sure enough, at anchor in the bay is the *Virago* itself, flying the skull and crossbones. Hearing a noise behind you, you look round to see four scurvy-looking characters advancing on you, weapons at the ready. 'You'll not be getting away this time,' sneers one of them and then the pirates charge at you. Fight them two at a time.

|                | SKILL | STAMINA |
|----------------|-------|---------|
| IORGA THE BEAR | 9     | 10      |
| BEASTFACE      | 8     | 8       |
| THE BOSUN      | 9     | 9       |
| ONE-EYED LAGAN | 10    | 7       |

If you defeat all your assailants, you decide that you have nothing to gain by trying to board the *Virago* and so set off for the Temple of Quezkari where you are sure the ritual to resurrect Cinnabar is to be completed. Turn to **115**.

## 11

The old wisewoman explains that to consult the spirits about your future you must give up some of your life-blood. If you agree to this, turn to **160**. If not, you will either have to choose that Madame Galbo heals your wounds (turn to **179**) or that she prepares a compound that might be of use to you on your quest (turn to **261**).

## 12

You hurl the powdered mixture in the undead pirate's face (cross it off your *Adventure Sheet*). The corpse's face distorts, not in pain but with laughter. 'You're going to need more than parlour tricks to stop Jolly Roger,' the macabre creature chuckles horribly. Turn to **147**.

## 13

The tunnel soon ends at a closed door. From beyond it, you hear the sound of something large moving around and there is an almost overpowering musky animal odour. Boldly, you fling open the door. The monster that is trapped inside the room immediately turns to face you. It looks like a huge predatory cat with a fiery red coat and mane, a ridge of spikes growing from its spine, and huge fangs. Lashing behind the beast are several long, snake-like tails, each ending in a stinging barb. This is truly a cat-o'-nine-tails! You are somehow going to have to get past this monster if you are to find the Pirates of the Black Skull. Do you want to attack it with your sword (turn to **78**) or will you try to distract the beast by throwing it some food (turn to **162**)?

## 14

You make your offering to the God of Pride (deduct the Gold Pieces from your *Adventure Sheet*). You automatically feel filled with renewed confidence and a sense of optimism. Vinar's blessing has been conferred upon you. Restore up to 2 LUCK points. Turn to **209**.

### 15

Captain Velyarde engages in combat with a lithe, well-dressed pirate while you find yourself challenged by a man built like a gorilla, and carrying a battle-axe. Hobbes, the *Virago's* First Mate, is a veteran of countless sea battles.

FIRST MATE HOBBES     SKILL 8     STAMINA 8

If you win, turn to **298**.

### 16

To try to avoid unwanted attention and in order to remain as inconspicuous as possible, you decide to wait until nightfall before investigating potential locations for the pirates' base. Add 2 Hours. Where will you begin your search? Around the docks (turn to **67**), at the ruined lighthouse on the promontory to the southeast of the port (turn to **146**), in the taverns and inns of the city (turn to **150**), in the sewers beneath the port (turn to **355**), at the cemetery outside the city walls (turn to **83**), or in the Temple Quarter (turn to **181**)?

## 17

You are passing a shop window containing a display of old maps and scrolls when you suddenly remember the cryptic message you overheard in the Gambling Pits, referring to Bone Island. Pausing, you take a closer look at the shop. Above the decorative window is a sign painted with the words: 'Mundi Pelago – Cartographer. Accurate and Attractive Maps and Charts.' Surely a mapmaker would be as good a person as any to ask about an island. Do you want to enter the shop (turn to **288**), or will you go on your way (turn to **334**)?

## 18

The stench of sulphur is too much for you and you misplace your next step. You land in the boiling mud and, before you can drag yourself out of the pool, manage to swallow some of it! Lose 2 STAMINA points and turn to **194**.

## 19

'Have it your own way,' Snide declares before leaving. Nobody comes to your cell that night, so you do not have an opportunity to bluff your way out of this predicament and the door is far too sturdy to break down. By the time you do get out of this dungeon you will be far too late to stop the Pirates of the Black Skull. Thanks to a grave injustice, you have failed in your mission.

## 20

Leaving the pygmies' lifeless bodies you continue further along the passageway, only to discover that it reaches a dead-end at a rock fall. It looks like the cave-in happened fairly recently. Do you want to see if you can shift some of the stones and force a way through the rock fall (turn to **140**) or would you rather return to the entrance to the temple and choose an alternative route (turn to **166**)?

## 21

Leaving the bats' chamber you continue along the tunnel. Suddenly your lantern illuminates a horrifying scene: a mouldering human skeleton hangs impaled on a row of spears that jut out from one wall of the tunnel. Too late you wonder if you may have strayed too far this time. The next second there is a whooshing, whistling sound and you react instantly. *Test your Skill*. If you succeed, turn to **196**. If you fail, turn to **138**.

## 22

'You must be joking!' laughs the guard. 'Now clear off before I forget I'm having a good day.' Do you want to persist in trying to enter the Old Fort (turn to **49**) or will you leave, if somewhat reluctantly, and go elsewhere (add 1 Hour and turn to **334**)?

## 23

Seeing you wielding the bone sword, Zyteea calls out, 'Nightdeath, aid us now!' Instantly, the blade glows with magical fire! You strike the thing with your curious weapon and it lets out a shrill cry of pain. Dropping the tribesman, the shadowy beast turns on you. Without further hesitation you attack the conjured voodoo spirit.

SPIRIT-BEAST          SKILL 10          STAMINA 12

If you win, turn to **277**.

## 24

As he leads you through the trees, Balinac tells you about his master. Apparently he was a wizard named Erasmus who lived in a secluded cell on the island. Originally the wizard came from a place called Halak in Allansia but he left the city to escape from the hustle and bustle of everyday life. You soon come to a small stone building in a clearing in the jungle, partially submerged in the earth. Inside, the place is in a state of disrepair and there is no sign of Erasmus. You ask Balinac where his master is and are surprised and confused by his reply: 'Master dead. Killed by voodoo man from skull face in the mountains. Balinac not go there.' Loping over to a straw-filled wooden box, Balinac says, 'Magical wine here. Master had magic books too,' and he points to a desk in one corner of the room. On it lie two weighty tomes, one entitled

the *Mythica* and the other the *Arcanum*. There might well be something here that could help you in your quest. Do you want to:

| | |
|---|---|
| Examine the potions? | Turn to **217** |
| Study the *Mythica*? | Turn to **47** |
| Read the *Arcanum*? | Turn to **5** |
| Leave the cell and Balinac? | Turn to **385** |

### 25

You step through the door and all too late notice a movement in the shadows either side of you. A heavy cosh hits you across the back of your head and you lose consciousness immediately. Turn to **158**.

### 26

The hold is illuminated by a phantasmal glow and as you look around you, the ghostly figures of the dead crew emerge from the shadows to surround you. Unable to escape, you wait for the undead's next move. The spectral sailors part and their cursed captain enters the ring. His eyes blaze like ship's lanterns and he wields a very real-looking, rusty cutlass in one hand. 'If you want to leave this ship,' he says in a booming voice like slamming crypt doors, 'you must best me, Captain Velyarde, in single combat. Unsheathe your weapon and prepare to fight!' With that, the ghost wildly attacks.

CAPTAIN VELYARDE     SKILL 10     STAMINA 10

If you win, turn to **395**.

## 27

Before you even reach Dead Men's Gate, a mass of figures emerge from out of the darkness and you are set upon by a crowd of pirates and black-robed Devotees. Soon overpowered, you are coshed over the head and knocked out. Turn to **158**.

## 28

Your attackers are Mask Zombies, created through dark voodoo rituals to be guards and servants in Quezkari's temple. The Zombies thrust at you with their flint-spears as you unsheathe your own weapon.

|  | SKILL | STAMINA |
|---|---|---|
| First MASK ZOMBIE | 8 | 6 |
| Second MASK ZOMBIE | 8 | 6 |

If you win, turn to **265**.

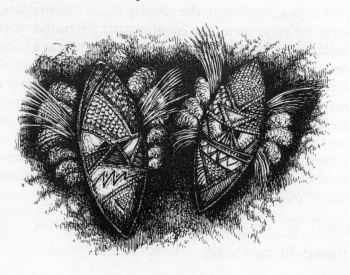

## 29

Despite being exquisitely made and incredibly detailed, there does not seem to be anything unusual about the ship. Of course, you could always try smashing the bottle to examine the model more closely, although this would probably make a lot of noise and possibly alert others on the ship to your presence. If you want to smash the bottle, turn to **293**. If not, will you:

| | |
|---|---|
| Look at the globe? | Turn to **349** |
| Open the chest? | Turn to **316** |
| Examine the desk? | Turn to **134** |
| Leave the cabin? | Turn to **233** |

## 30

Your battle over, you suddenly find yourself surrounded by Mask Zombies. Unable to take on all of the Voodoo Priest's undead slaves you soon find yourself restrained and dragged from the Scarachna's web-lair. Hauled into the inner sanctum of the temple, you are brought before Ramatu, the High Priest of Quezkari. At one end of the chamber is a statue of the voodoo death-god, just as in the shrine back in the Port of Crabs, only this one is even larger and more macabre. The High Priest himself is an intimidating figure. He wears crimson and scarlet robes, no doubt dyed in blood, a feathered headdress like that of Quezkari and a necklace of shrunken human heads. On his chest is the tattoo of a huge black skull, and in one hand he is holding an up-turned human skull full of a foul green liquid.

'Intruder,' he says, speaking for the first time, 'you have trespassed within the Temple of the Dark One. As punishment, you must drink the Ichor of Quezkari!' Held in the tight grip of the Mask Zombies your mouth is forced open and the foul liquid is poured down your throat and you are made to swallow. Immediately you are assailed by all manner of phantasmal creatures; cruel jeering spirits and grotesque half-human things. *Test your Skill*. If you fail, turn to **62**. If you succeed, turn to **248**.

## 31

Gulping down the potion, you grab hold of the portcullis with both hands and heave! Disregard the bonus the potion normally adds to your Attack Strength and turn to **99**.

## 32

You do not have to wait long for your turn. (Deduct 2 Gold Pieces from your *Adventure Sheet*.) Eagle-eyed, you watch closely as the man shows you where the white card is and then places all the cards face down on the table. He deftly switches their positions at an incredible speed, but you keep concentrating on the white card. When he finally stops, you point to the card you are sure is the white one. With a smile, Armarno turns it over and reveals it to be black. You have a sneaking suspicion that the Amazing Armarno is conning you. Do you want to challenge the trickster about this suspected fraud (turn to **258**), play another game, just to be sure (turn to **118**) or will you move on from this stand (turn to **223**)?

## 33

Running hell-for-leather, you round a corner and run straight into more of Cinnabar's pirates. You are soon overcome. Receiving a blow to the back of your head from a heavy cosh, you lose consciousness... Turn to **158**.

## 34

Your weapon is taken from you and you are taken to a pit into which you are lowered while a bamboo gate on the other side is raised. Instantly, a snarling Jaguar springs into the pit and lashes out at you with its claws. Unarmed, you must wrestle the predatory cat with your SKILL reduced by 2 points for this fight.

JAGUAR                    SKILL 8        STAMINA 7

However, if you win two consecutive Attack Rounds, or reduce the Jaguar's STAMINA to 2 points or less, turn to **394**. If the cat reduces your STAMINA score to 3 points or less first, the Jaguar is held at bay and you are rescued from the pit and have your weapon returned (turn to **194**).

### 35

You manage to dodge the pan of scalding water as it sails past your head. But now you are going to have to deal with the enraged Bladderwrack. A meat cleaver gripped tightly in one podgy hand, the cannibal cook charges at you, his rolls of fat wobbling disgustingly.

BLADDERWRACK THE
   COOK           SKILL 8      STAMINA 10

If you defeat the cook, turn to **285**.

### 36

Pulling back the pirate flag you prise open the nailed lid of the coffin. You gasp and take a step back on seeing that the coffin is still occupied. Lying within is the body of a pirate still wearing a tricorn hat and ragged waistcoat. The dead man's hands are crossed on his chest, and in its rigour mortis-locked fingers the corpse clutches a golden talisman fashioned to look like a scorpion. The most peculiar thing about the pirate's corpse is that despite being trapped within a sealed coffin and left in an abandoned room, apart from having a rather unhealthy grey pallor to its skin, it does not look like it has really begun to decay at all. What will you do now? Do you want to take the Scorpion Talisman from the corpse (turn to **89**), or would you rather leave this unsettling place (turn to **166**)?

## 37

There is a rustling amongst the frond-like leaves of a tree in front of you and suddenly you find yourself looking into two yellow eyes, with black slits for pupils. You stop and stare as an angular green face emerges from amidst the vegetation. You are facing a tiny humanoid with cat-like eyes and spindly, twig-like limbs. The little creature is wearing a startling headdress of parakeet feathers, a grass skirt and is holding a javelin in one bony hand. The tiny humanoid puts its head on one side and smiles broadly at you before holding out its empty hand towards you. How will you respond to this action? Will you:

| | |
|---|---|
| Offer the creature some food? | Turn to 348 |
| Give the creature an item from your backpack? | Turn to 122 |
| Attack the creature? | Turn to 307 |
| Ignore the creature and go on your way? | Turn to 384 |

Rubbing the serrated edges of the teeth against the rope, with the bracelet on your wrist, you soon cut through the strands. You free yourself just before the water filling the pit covers your head. Climbing out of a potentially watery grave, you find your back-pack and sword dumped nearby – nothing has been taken (regain 1 LUCK point). Without further delay, hurriedly you head off after the pirates. You soon find yourself at the edge of a huge natural cavern, inside which the sea has formed a large bay. At the far end of the cave is an entrance large enough to admit a sailing vessel. And sure enough, moored to a jetty at the edge of the water, is a great galleon. The ship flies the skull and crossbones flag common to all pirate vessels and instead of a figurehead, you are disturbed to see a human skeleton bound to the bowsprit. Before you see the name *Virago* painted on its side you know that this is Cinnabar's galleon which was supposed to have sunk. You can see the Pirates of the Black Skull milling around on the deck, but there is no-one left on the jetty – the *Virago* must be ready to sail. Keeping yourself hidden in the shadows of the cave, you watch as the anchor is raised and Cinnabar's galleon starts to make its way out to sea. Then you see a way to stop your quarry escaping you. A porthole in the side of the ship has been left open and a knotted rope hangs down from the deck next to it. Quickly you make a dash for the jetty and, remaining unspotted, climb the rope, slipping silently in through the opening.

You find yourself inside a small, disused storeroom. You decide to lay low here for a while before exploring the ship. Stowed away on board you watch through the porthole as the *Virago* leaves the Port of Crabs behind under cover of darkness. When you are sure the coast is clear you creep out of the room into a corridor. To your right is a door with the brass plaque 'Captain' fixed to it. At the far end of the corridor a staircase descends into the galleon. Another passage runs off from the first to your left, with a door at its far end and two unmarked doors to the left and right. Will you:

| | |
|---|---|
| Open the far door? | Turn to **191** |
| Open the door to the left? | Turn to **127** |
| Open the door to the right? | Turn to **141** |
| Open the door marked 'Captain'? | Turn to **97** |
| Descend the staircase? | Turn to **211** |

**39**

Inhaling great lungfuls of the smoke you start to think that you can see skeletal faces hovering around you, filling you with a sense of enormous unease. You sweep at the apparitions with your sword, but to no avail. These are horrors of your own imagining and cannot be harmed by physical weapons. Afflicted by this terrible, paranoid fear, while you remain in the temple you must reduce your SKILL by 1 point. Turn to **185**.

## 40

As you approach the gate, out of the corner of your eye you notice a movement in a darkened alleyway. Instantly, two figures step out into the street in front of you. One is a gaunt-looking character, holding a cruel sabre and with a frayed noose around his neck. The other is an attractive Khulian woman with her long, shining, black hair twisted into a plait, wearing finely-made leather armour and wielding a thin sword. You recognise the first of your assailants from tales you have heard on your travels. He is the notorious pirate Silas Gallows. His companion is Wu-Lin, a mercenary who joined Cinnabar's crew not long before the pirate-lord was killed. Both bear the insignia of the Pirates of the Black Skull. 'So here we are at Dead Men's Gate,' chuckles Silas Gallows, 'and soon there's gonna be one more corpse in Corpse Way!' Wu-Lin says nothing but advances towards you, her gleaming blade raised. Fight them both at the same time.

|  | SKILL | STAMINA |
|---|---|---|
| SILAS GALLOWS | 7 | 7 |
| WU-LIN | 8 | 6 |

If you win, not wanting to meet any more of Cinnabar's cronies, you hurry out of the city. Turn to **119**.

## 41

'Ho ho, yes that'll do nicely,' chuckles the castaway, and proceeds to tell you that the treasure is hidden in a system of caves west of his camp. 'Mind you,' Scrimshaw adds, 'Blackscar's hoard is cursed. Those are pearls that were his eyes. Any thief who tries to steal it will get all they deserve. Don't say I didn't warn you.' With that the mad old man skips off, pleased with his present, ignoring you completely. Will you now set off to find Blackscar's treasure (turn to 110) or look for signs of Cinnabar's pirates (turn to 208)?

## 42

You are enticed towards the Bazaar by its colourful stalls, as well as the sounds and smells of far-off countries. You ignore the rolls of silk and the baskets of spices but are attracted to a brightly decorated stall covered in a variety of unusual items. Talking with the vendor, you discover that the man is a Talismonger – a trader in artefacts that are allegedly magical. However, by the look of some of the objects, you do wonder if they really are charged with esoteric power. The magical items the Talismonger has on offer are listed below with their prices. You may buy as many of them as you want, as long as you have enough Gold Pieces.

| Ivory Lion Charm | 7 Gold Pieces | Turn to 301 |
| Shark's Teeth Bracelet | 5 Gold Pieces | Turn to 170 |
| Magical Compass | 9 Gold Pieces | Turn to 59 |
| Potion of Giant-Strength | 8 Gold Pieces | Turn to 374 |
| Lock of Elvin's Hair | 6 Gold Pieces | Turn to 165 |
| Carved Darkwood Armband | 4 Gold Pieces | Turn to 399 |

Once you have made your purchases, turn to 200.

## 43

The combination of the noise from your battle and the shrieks of the bats amplified by the echoing chamber cause several of the stalactites to crack and fall from the roof. You are immediately caught in a rockfall. Roll one dice, add 2 to the roll and deduct the total from your STAMINA score. If you survive the cave-in will you risk going further into the caves (turn to **21**) or turn back and give up on finding Blackscar's treasure (turn to **279**)?

## 44

You suddenly realise what the Witchdoctor is up to: he is trying to cloud your mind with magic. Concentrating hard, you step into the chalk circle, breaking Malu's spell. Almost on top of the man, you cannot avoid combat as he springs to his feet and lunges at you with his wand.

MALU THE
  WITCHDOCTOR        SKILL 9      STAMINA 8

If the Witchdoctor strikes you, the wand drains 3 points of STAMINA from you rather than the usual 2. If you kill Cinnabar's servant, turn to **366**.

## 45

Although you cut down several of the Zombies, ultimately there are too many of them for one warrior to vanquish alone. Your adventure is over.

## 46

Grasping you with its powerful limbs, the Octopus employs its favourite tactic of squeezing the life from its prey. Lose an additional point of STAMINA. Held in the monster's vice-like grip, unless you can break free by winning the next Attack Round, you will suffer the crushing damage again, which will increase by a further point each time. Return to **280** and continue your struggle with the Octopus.

## 47

The well-thumbed tome is actually a book of myths and legends. Flicking through it your eye is caught by one page in particular, which has the name 'Quezkari' written at the top. You read with interest about the evil voodoo spirit and find a section describing wards used to protect against Quezkari's power. The text refers to a Spirit Jewel and a magical bone weapon rumoured to be hidden in a cave system somewhere on the island! Now do you want to:

| | |
|---|---|
| Examine the potions? | Turn to **217** |
| Study the *Arcanum*? | Turn to **5** |
| Leave Erasmus's cell? | Turn to **385** |

## 48

Continuing along the passageway, you follow it as it turns right and reaches a junction. The passage you are in soon comes to a dead-end in a chamber in which is the bizarre statue of some kind of lizard. The new tunnel bends round to the left after a few metres so you cannot see what lies along it. Will you enter the statue room (turn to **88**) or take the new path (turn to **295**)?

## 49

At once the guard pulls a chain which sets off a jangling of bells inside the fort. Almost immediately, the gates open and what seems like half the City Guard pour out to surround you. Turn to **236**.

## 50

When you have completed your tale, the Queen speaks: 'Your cause is a noble one but we have had dealings with the cult of Quezkari ourselves. How do we know that you are not lying to us in order to ensnare us to the Evil One? We must be sure. You must take the Test of the Warrior.' If these people are to trust you, and you gain their help, you can't deny Queen Zyteea's decree. You are led to a pool of

bubbling mud. Sulphurous fumes rise from it and a tree trunk has been laid across the middle. You are then blindfolded and told to walk across the log! Judging your position by touch alone and your head spinning from the fumes, you take your first step. *Test your Skill* twice, adding 1 to the roll each time. If you pass both tests, turn to **259**. If you fail either of them, turn to **18**.

### 51

Do you have the word 'Regnad' written on your *Adventure Sheet*? If so, turn to **310**. If not, turn to **287**.

### 52

Choosing somewhere you've not been yet, where will you continue your search?

| | |
|---|---|
| The docks? | Turn to **67** |
| The ruined lighthouse? | Turn to **146** |
| The taverns and inns? | Turn to **150** |
| The sewers? | Turn to **355** |
| The cemetery? | Turn to **83** |
| The Temple Quarter? | Turn to **181** |

### 53

The jungle in front of you suddenly appears to move and then a huge, lizard-like shape melts out of the greenery. The Giant Chameleon focuses on you with its bizarre, rotating eyes and moves jerkily towards you. Riding on its back is a humanoid chameleon-like creature wielding a short spear. The gigantic lizard hisses and its scales take on a variety of brilliant hues

– a sure sign that it is angry and about to attack. Once again you are fighting for your life!

GIANT CHAMELEON      SKILL 9      STAMINA 9

If the Giant Chameleon's Attack Strength is over 20 or 21, and it wins the Attack Round, turn to **133**. If you kill the lizard, the Chameleonite riding it escapes into the jungle, its camouflaged skin keeping it safe from detection. Add the word 'Depacse' to your *Adventure Sheet* and turn to the paragraph with the number you noted down earlier.

### 54

You tread water for several hours, but no ships come in sight. Exhausted, the sea finally claims you for its own.

### 55

You have wasted enough time here already, so you prepare to leave the Silent Donkey. *Test your Luck.* If you are Lucky, turn to **218**. If you are Unlucky, turn to **25**.

## 56

'Stranger,' says one of the warriors, in a language you can understand, 'leave our village. You are not welcome here.' If you do as the warrior commands, turn to **164**. If you want to persist in trying to enter the tribespeople's village, turn to **206**.

## 57

Following the passageway right past the T-junction, you pass between walls crudely daubed with images of Quezkari and other voodoo deities dealing out death in its various forms to humans. Feeling the floor shift, you immediately know what is happening: a balance trap has been triggered and the floor is tilting up to reveal a deep, spiked pit underneath it. Your only hope is to leap over the treacherous gap now opening up before you. *Test your Skill*. If you succeed, turn to **308**. If you fail, turn to **240**.

## 58

You slowly become aware of a fluttering sound in the air behind you. You spin round to see a huge fanged bat flapping towards you. It is the spirit of the vanquished Jolly Roger. The vampire has returned to feast on your blood so that it might restore itself to true unlife. You are going to have to fight the bat if you are to escape from this chamber.

BLOODTHIRSTY BAT     SKILL 7     STAMINA 5

If the bat scores two successive hits against you, it rips at your throat with its distended fangs causing you to lose 3 STAMINA points, rather than the usual 2. If you defeat Jolly Roger's undead spirit for a second time you flee the chamber without a second thought. Turn to **166**.

### 59

The Talismonger tells you that the lodestone inside the compass is attracted to large deposits of gold – a must for any would-be treasure hunter. It is only after you have handed over your money that you wonder why the Talismonger hasn't used the compass himself to make *his* fortune. Return to **42**.

### 60

As the rest of the crew repel the other Crabs, the ship starts to list to one side. The crustaceans must have actually holed the hull. With the *Fortune* so badly damaged, you will not be able to pursue Cinnabar and can only look forward to a future as crab food. Your adventure is over.

### 61

How many Gold Pieces are you offering? If it is less than 5 Gold Pieces, turn to **22**; otherwise, turn to **195**.

### 62

The hallucinations continue and become too much for you. With a hysterical scream, you lose your mind through fear. With no longer any will of your own, you become one of those whom you have so desperately tried to destroy – a devotee of the Black Skull and a servant of Evil. Your adventure is over.

## 63

You are half way across the bridge when one of the rotten planks from which it is comprised suddenly splinters and gives way under your weight. *Test your Skill*. If you succeed, turn to **273**. If you fail, turn to **317**.

## 64

Despite having a wooden leg, the old rogue moves quite quickly and disappears around a corner before you can catch up with him. As you are about to round the corner yourself, you suddenly start to have misgivings about your latest course of action. Will you continue to follow the pirate (turn to **282**) or go back the way you have just come (turn to **266**)?

## 65

Wandering over the barren terrain you keep an eye out for any sign of Cinnabar's cronies or evidence of buried treasure. *Test your Luck* twice. If you are Lucky both times, turn to **110**. If you are Unlucky either time, turn to **208**.

## 66

There is no sign of another human soul having been washed up on the island so, sadly, you assume that you were the only survivor of the Behemoth's attack. Even the famed bounty-hunter Conyn is gone. Mourning the loss of the *Fortune*, you continue to wander south along the shore-line. Rounding a sandy promontory you are surprised by what you see before you. Ten metres away, a primitive human-like creature, with strongly muscled arms and covered in red hair, is tearing open some of the crates washed up from the wreck. The creature looks up, hearing you approach, and growls. Will you:

| | |
|---|---|
| Prepare to defend yourself? | Turn to **95** |
| Make a run for it into the jungle? | Turn to **125** |
| Try to communicate with the creature? | Turn to **358** |
| Offer the primitive something? | Turn to **183** |

## 67

The docks are quiet at this time of night. You decide that if the pirates' hideout was located around the docks, the entrance would have to be in the harbour wall somewhere. Descending to the wooden jetties, you start your search. *Thud*. What was that? *Thud*. There it is again. You stand perfectly still, your ears straining to pick up any sound. Then you hear the rattling of a chain being dragged across the wooden planks close by. *Swoosh!* A large anchor suddenly flies out of the dense mist, in a sweeping arc, towards you.

*Test your Luck.* If you are Lucky, turn to **321**. If you are Unlucky, turn to **230**.

## 68

The tropical environment of the island is very different to the northerly, wind-lashed Port of Crabs. The day drags on as you stagger through the jungle, your clothes soaked with sweat. Entering a low valley, you come upon a scene of utter devastation. In a large clearing lies what is left of a tribespeople's village. The place has been razed to the ground and a deathly silence hangs over the place. Do you want to quickly pass through the ruined village (turn to **197**) or would you rather pause here and explore it (turn to **117**)?

## 69

As soon as you have stepped underneath the portcullis it drops down, blocking the way out! There is nothing in the cave of any use to you, so you set about trying to get out again. There is no chain or lever inside the cave to raise the portcullis, so you decide that you will have to resort to brute force. If you have a Potion of Giant-Strength, you may drink it now (turn to **31**). If you do not have the potion, or you do not want to use it, turn to **120**.

## 70

You open the door and find yourself in the pirates' shrine to their dark god, dominated by a hideous statue of the skeletal Quezkari, but the place is empty. You are too late! Cinnabar and his crew have already left this place and, unable to follow them, you have failed in your quest.

## 71

You gasp in shock as you hit the freezing water and disappear beneath the surface of the pool. Feeling your way forwards under the water, you find an opening in the rock wall. Swimming through it you emerge inside another cave. Glowing crystals placed around the cavern provide light to see by, which is reflected off glinting gold coins and the facets of precious jewels. You have never seen such a fabulous hoard. Lying, almost discarded, to one side of the treasure pile is a curious sword-like weapon carved from bone! Do you want to:

| | |
|---|---|
| Take a closer look at the bone weapon? | Turn to **306** |
| Collect some of the gold and jewels? | Turn to **123** |
| Leave Blackscar's 'cursed' treasure untouched? | Turn to **279** |

## 72

Filled with an overwhelming sense of foreboding, you hurriedly return to the deck and depart the *Sea Maiden*. Lose 1 LUCK point and turn to **153**.

## 73

The Octopus sinks back under the waves, its foul blood staining the water purple. Confident that it will now be safe to explore the cave, you do just that but, to your disappointment, find no other tunnels leading from it. The pirates' hideout obviously isn't here. Turn to **350**.

## 74

Swinging their cudgels, the pirates engage you in combat.

|  | SKILL | STAMINA |
|---|---|---|
| First PIRATE | 7 | 7 |
| Second PIRATE | 6 | 7 |

If you win, the Half-Ogre steps forward to fight you. Will you face your opponent (turn to **187**) or try to escape (turn to **6**)?

## 75

The undead pirate smashes the gem from your hand and it shatters on the stone floor of the chamber. Cross the Blue Gem off your *Adventure Sheet* and turn to **147**.

## 76

Overcome with fear you fling open the door and rush out of the room. You have been badly shaken by your experience (lose 1 SKILL point and 1 LUCK point). Will you now:

| | |
|---|---|
| Open the left-hand door? | Turn to **353** |
| Enter the hold? | Turn to **26** |
| Leave the *Sea Maiden*? | Turn to **153** |

## 77

The two monsters snap, slash and hurl themselves at each other as you watch, transfixed. Run the fight between the ape and the lizard, rolling for Attack Strengths and deducting STAMINA points, as you would if you were fighting either of the creatures.

|  | SKILL | STAMINA |
|---|---|---|
| GREAT APE | 8 | 10 |
| TERRIBLE LIZARD | 7 | 11 |

As soon as one of the colossi has defeated the other, turn to **205**.

## 78

With a roar, the mutant bounds towards you. You have no choice but to fight the monster.

NINE-TAILS      SKILL 10     STAMINA 10

The cat attacks by trying to slash you with its great claws and bite you with its huge fangs. However, if the monster hits you, roll one dice. If you roll 6, the beast has hit you with its barbed tails instead: roll one dice and deduct the number rolled from your STAMINA score. You may *Test your Luck* to avoid this damage if you wish. Keep track of how much STAMINA you lose in this way. If you survive this battle, turn to **235**.

## 79

Scrambling up the galleon's rigging, you find yourself trapped, unless... Cutting a rope free, you grab hold of the end and leap into mid-air. Swinging down towards the pirates you flail about with your sword to keep them at bay. There is a cry of pain from one of the buccaneers and you see a red-haired woman clutching the stump where her hand used to be. You sail past the infuriated pirates over the edge of the *Virago*. Letting go of the rope, you drop several metres before hitting the water. The galleon continues on its course, leaving you stranded in the middle of the Western Ocean, as the crew watch you, laughing. Or are they really looking at you? They actually seem to be watching something behind you. 'Have a good swim!' shouts one of them. Turning round in the water you see the tell-tale triangular fin and, ducking your head under the waves, you see the Great White Shark closing in on you, jaws wide open. You just have time to draw your sword before it is on you.

GREAT WHITE SHARK     SKILL 9     STAMINA 10

Fighting underwater is difficult and as a result you must reduce your Attack Strength by 2 points for the duration of this battle. Also, unless you defeat the Shark in less Attack Rounds than your current SKILL score you will drown! If you kill the Great White, turn to **186**.

## 80

The tunnel winds its way into the hill until it opens into a high-ceilinged chamber, with stalactites pointing down from the cave roof. A piercing squeaking starts up as, disturbed by the light from your lantern, three large bats flap down from their roosts to drive you off. As the creatures batter you with their wings, you catch a glimpse of their greatly enlarged front teeth. You must fight the Vampire Bats.

|  | SKILL | STAMINA |
|---|---|---|
| First VAMPIRE BAT | 5 | 4 |
| Second VAMPIRE BAT | 5 | 5 |
| Third VAMPIRE BAT | 5 | 4 |

While you are fighting one of the screeching bats, those remaining land on you and suck your blood, each causing 1 STAMINA point of damage per Attack Round. If you kill all three, turn to **148**.

## 81

The Arrow of Providence is a popular game of chance in the Gambling Pits. It is made up of a large circular board divided into twelve sections, each painted with a legend. An arrow-like pointer has been attached to the centre of the board so that it can be spun. To play the game will cost 2 Gold Pieces but you will be playing for a potential jackpot of 10 Gold Pieces. If you want to play, turn to **346**. If you do not want to have a go, you leave the Arrow of Providence (turn to **260**).

## 82

Deep down you know that the nightmares you are witnessing are not real and manage to convince yourself that they are merely illusions. At once the phantasms vanish. However, Ramatu is obviously expecting you to be overcome by fear and, surrounded by Zombies, you are in no position to stop him. In a brilliant piece of acting, you let out a loud scream and collapse on the floor. Satisfied that he has broken your will, Ramatu dismisses the Mask Zombies and returns to his blasphemous rituals. When you are sure the coast is clear, you leap to your feet and run at the High Priest, yelling. If you have the word 'Dehsams' written on your *Adventure Sheet*, turn to 324. If not, turn to 139.

## 83

Keeping to shadowy doorways wherever possible, you make your way swiftly along Corpse Way towards Dead Men's Gate. Do you have any of the following words written on your *Adventure Sheet*: 'Etarip', 'Rohcna', 'Yeknod' or 'Desruc'? Count up the number of words you have noted down from the list above and if you have:

| | |
|---|---|
| None of the words. | Turn to 119 |
| One or two of the words. | Turn to 40 |
| Three or four of the words. | Turn to 27 |

## 84

Your reactions are not quick enough and the gobbet of silk hits you, sticking fast. Before you can cut yourself free, a second strand squirts from the monster's jaws and your sword-arm is fixed to your side. In no time at all, you are trapped inside a cocoon of silk, trussed up in a tree and left in the spider-scorpion's larder until it feels like a snack. Your adventure is over.

## 85

As you are hacking your way through the dense undergrowth you unwittingly disturb the sensitive carpet of vines surrounding the vase-like trunk of a Giant Pitcher-Plant. A strong tendril suddenly whips out of the jungle and you find yourself fighting for your life against the carnivorous plant.

TENDRIL            SKILL 8       STAMINA 7

If the tendril wins three consecutive Attack Rounds, turn immediately to 383. If you defeat the tendril without this happening, turn to 343.

## 86

Poison darts shoot out of the walls just above your head, missing you by millimetres. You were lucky this time but from now on you'll have to be more careful. Turn to 48.

## 87

Caught unawares, you are unable to avoid the effects of the Witchdoctor's magic: your mind becomes confused and addled. The man takes advantage of your befuddled state and springs at you, using his wand as his weapon.

MALU THE
     WITCHDOCTOR      SKILL 9       STAMINA 8

For the duration of this battle you must reduce your Attack Strength by 2 points. If the Witchdoctor strikes you, the wand drains 3 points of STAMINA from you rather than the usual 2. If you kill Cinnabar's servant, turn to **366**.

## 88

The bronze iguana-like creature, green with age, stands three metres tall on its hindlegs with its mouth open and has sparkling diamonds for eyes. Apart from the worrying bloodstains on the floor, there is nothing else of interest here, so will you leave the chamber and take the other tunnel (turn to **295**) or first try to prise the diamonds from their sockets (turn to **176**)?

## 89

Prising the dead pirate's fingers open, you try to take the talisman from the corpse. Suddenly the dead man's eyes flick open and a cruel smile twists its drawn lips, revealing the elongated points of the pirate's incisors. You leap backwards in fright, feeling badly shaken (lose 1 LUCK point). You are going to have to act quickly. Will you draw your sword (turn to **147**), look for something else to use from your backpack (turn to **108**) or attempt to flee (turn to **276**)?

## 90

'Ah, Bone Island,' muses Conyn. 'I've heard rumours about the place. Talk of voodoo and buried treasure, but I didn't know of its location until now.' Before directing his crew to set a course for Bone Island, Conyn turns to you. 'There are two different routes we can take. The quicker one should allow us to catch up with the *Virago* but will take us through the Crab Reefs, which are notorious for the gigantic crustaceans said to dwell there. However, if we avoid the reefs our journey will take longer. Which way do you think we should go? Through the Crab Reefs (turn to 267) or around them (turn to 297)?'

## 91

You pass several recessed, grilled doors through which are cramped, dank cells, their only inhabitants creeping, slithering things and the yellowed bones of former prisoners. At the end of the passage you enter a large cave-like chamber with more doors leading from it. However, standing on guard are two peculiar figures. Their flesh is grey and withered and their faces are covered by primitive tribal masks. Each holds a spear and on seeing you they move towards you. Will you fight the guards (turn to 28) or run for it back down the tunnel and past the T-junction (turn to 57)?

## 92

Boldly, you speak the word, 'Leviathan'. Turn to **269**.

## 93

You draw your sword and thrust it in the old man's face, but this merely makes him laugh all the more. Sniggering like the simpleton he is, Scrimshaw sprints away into the hills, leaving you to explore them without his help. Turn to **65**.

## 94

You hare off through the jungle, the Great Ape's bellowing cries fading into the echoing distance behind you. Turn to the paragraph with the number you noted down previously.

## 95

Seeing you draw your sword, the creature goes berserk. Baring its teeth, it leaps at you snarling, 'Balinac kill!' You have no choice but to fight the primitive Balinac.

BALINAC        SKILL 8      STAMINA 8

If you kill the apeman, you search through the crates and find nothing but rotting foodstuffs. Balinac has no possessions so you decide to set off into the jungle in the hope of still stopping Cinnabar's pirates. Turn to **125**.

## 96

'Nightdeath, aid me now!' you cry and the bone blade bursts into flame. Screeching, Quezkari attacks. The voodoo death-god is actually a powerful, evil spirit – a manifestation of the souls of all those transformed into Zombies by the evil Ramatu and those killed by Cinnabar. If you have a Wristband of White Feathers, the courage of the Usai people is with you as you fight (add 1 to your Attack Strength).

QUEZKARI        SKILL 13     STAMINA 18

Each time Quezkari wounds you his dark powers drain 3 STAMINA points from you, unless you are protected by the Ivory Lion Charm, in which case you only lose the usual 2. If you overcome all the odds and defeat the all-powerful spirit, turn to **400**.

## 97

As you suspected, the door opens into the Captain's cabin. Fortunately, however, there is no sign of anyone being here at the moment. The cabin is plushly decorated with mahogany panelling and thick velvet drapes. The room is lit by an oil lamp hanging from a beam and an empty birdcage swings from the rafters, but there are four things that really attract your attention: a globe of Titan, a large oak chest, Cinnabar's desk and an ornate ship in a bottle. If you don't want to take a closer look at any of these, turn to **233**. If you do, which will it be?

| | |
|---|---|
| The globe? | Turn to **349** |
| The chest? | Turn to **316** |
| The desk? | Turn to **134** |
| The ship in a bottle? | Turn to **29** |

## 98

The fortune-teller remains silent as you drop your money into his pot. Without looking up, he turns over the first card at the top of the deck. On it is painted the picture of a black skull! You immediately feel a chill in your veins and a forbidding atmosphere of evil pressing down on you. In anger and fear you draw your sword and strike the man. At your blow, the rags collapse in a heap – there is no sign of anyone ever having been there! (Lose 2 LUCK points and add the word 'Desruc' to your *Adventure Sheet*.) Panicked, you turn and flee through the Temple Quarter, only stopping again when you have put many streets between you and the wise men. Add 1 Hour and turn to **334**.

## 99

You manage to raise the portcullis far enough to get out of the cave and then make for the door instead. Carefully, you open the second door. How long has it taken you to get this far? If it has taken 9 Hours or more, turn to **70**. If it has taken 8 Hours or less, turn to **333**.

## 100

Madame Galbo's cottage is an unassuming building in the quiet Mandrake's Lane, although somewhat disturbing is the votive totem, made from a dead bird's carcass, nailed to the door. You knock three times and, hearing a croaky 'Enter!', push open the door. You immediately find yourself in a herbalist's paradise; bunches of herbs hang from the low rafters of the room, which is filled with a profusion of potted plants. The greenery and humidity of the chamber make you feel like you are in the depths of a tropical rainforest. Sitting behind a cluttered table is a dark-skinned old woman with a crumpled face and thick curly black hair – Madame Galbo. The wisewoman is busy preparing a concoction in a pestle and mortar. As you enter the room, there is a great squawking and flapping at your feet as a large black cockerel hops out of your way. 'Don't mind Rabab,' says Madame Galbo of her familiar. 'Now what can I do for you?' You sense that you can trust this woman so you tell her of your search for the Pirates of the Black Skull. 'The followers of the Dark One have many guises and set many traps to ensnare the unwary. If you are to confront them you will need my help for I have an understanding of the ways of voodoo and can do something to counteract it. But assistance comes at a price – four Gold Pieces.' If you can afford this amount, and you are prepared to pay for the wise-woman's help, turn to **382**. If not, you will have to leave Madame Galbo's cottage to look elsewhere for a means of defeating Cinnabar's cronies (turn to **239**).

The Silent Donkey is situated on a dingy back street within the Claws. Several suspicious characters watch you enter the inn but none try to stop you. Creeping up the creaky wooden staircase, you come to the first room on the first floor – room 101. The key turns in the lock and, opening the door, you step into a room furnished with only a table and chair. But what you see there sends an icy chill down your spine. On the table rests a human skull, painted black and decorated with a headdress of brightly coloured bird's feathers. The Black Skull! This is a bad omen. There is nobody here so this must have all been a set-up by Cinnabar's cronies to delay you! The skull fills you with foreboding but it still intrigues you. If you want to take it with you, turn to **244**; if not, turn to **55**.

### 102

The bolt hits you in the thigh making you stumble and fall onto the wooden planks. Lose 2 STAMINA points, and in the battle to come for the first Attack Round reduce your Attack Strength by 2 points as you try to get up again. Turn to **182**.

### 103

The Old Fort, residence of the Governor of the Port of Crabs, stands at the top of the hill on which most of the Old Town Quarter of the city is built. You climb the hill and arrive outside the grim stone building. The whole edifice looks like it could withstand an army's onslaught for weeks, even though it is now several centuries old. As you approach the guard at the gate, he asks you your business, and you demand an audience with Governor Montargo. 'Oh yeah?' sneers the guard. 'I can't let just anyone in 'ere, can I. It's more than my job's worth.' If you want to try bribing him, decide how many Gold Pieces you will offer the guard and then turn to **61**. Alternatively you could threaten him with cold steel (turn to **49**). If you don't want to try either of these options you will have to leave (add 1 Hour and turn to **334**).

## 104

The crystal explodes in a blaze of light, blasting shards of rock around the chamber, but incredibly you manage to get away fairly unscathed! (Lose 2 STAMINA points.) There is nothing more you can do here so you leave the crystal room. Record the word 'Dehsams' on your *Adventure Sheet* and turn to **329**.

## 105

The second blow knocks you off your feet. Before you can get up again, the Anchor Man quickly loops the heavy chain round your ankles and throws the anchor far out into the harbour. You are immediately dragged from the pier, into the sea, and pulled underwater as the anchor rapidly sinks towards the floor of the harbour. Only just controlling the urge to panic, you try to free yourself from the chain. Roll two dice and add 12. If the total is less than or equal to your STAMINA score, turn to **340**; if it is greater, turn to **249**.

## 106

You shake the wand at the unearthly creature, but to no effect. As you are doing this Quezkari lashes out at you with a taloned hand (lose 2 STAMINA points). You have no choice now but to retaliate with your sword. Turn to **177**.

## 107

Unable to escape, you face a slow, agonizing death at the hands of Cinnabar's sadistic torturer. You have failed in your quest and your adventure is most definitely over.

### 108

If you have any of the following you have time to try to use one of them against the risen pirate. Will you choose:

| | |
|---|---|
| Zombie Dust? | Turn to **12** |
| A skeleton artefact? | Turn to **356** |
| A broken balustrade? | Turn to **189** |
| A blue gem? | Turn to **75** |
| A witchdoctor's wand? | Turn to **212** |

If you do not have any of the above items, or choose not to use any of them, turn to **147**.

### 109

As you elbow your way through the bustling crowds, above the hubbub you hear a gruff voice say in a harsh whisper, 'The *Virago* sails for Bone Island at midnight.' Looking round you see two knavish-looking characters part company and go their separate ways among the throng. You will not be able to follow them now. The *Virago* was the name of Cinnabar's ship and what was that about an island? This careless talk could be an important clue (write down the word 'Dnalsi' on your *Adventure Sheet*). Will you now move on to Calabrius's Calculator (turn to **294**), visit 'The Amazing Armarno' (turn to **9**) or leave the Gambling Pits (turn to **207**)?

### 110

Eventually you come to a wide cave entrance at the foot of a rocky escarpment. Inside, a tunnel leads off into the darkness. You will need to use your lantern if

you are to enter the caverns. If you want to do just that, turn to **80**. If not, you decide to head northeast, back into the island's interior (turn to **279**).

### 111

(Add 1 Hour to your total.) As you are walking along Traders Street away from the market, you cannot help but notice a roguish figure standing on the corner of Lobster Alley. The man is gaunt and scrawny, in his later years, and with several days' growth of stubble. He also has an eye-patch, a wooden stump for a leg beneath his right knee and wears a long coat and tricorn hat. A monkey, with its own tiny waistcoat, is scampering around the man's shoulders. As you walk past the pirate, you make eye contact and he beckons to you with a glance before turning and hobbling away up the alley. Will you follow the man (turn to **64**) or go on your way (turn to **143**)?

### 112

The Scarachna's sting lashes forwards and strikes you, sending its toxic venom coursing through your body. (Lose 6 STAMINA points.) If you survive this attack, turn back to **201** and continue your battle.

### 113

You are led to the largest hut in the village where you are brought before a lithe, beautiful woman dressed like the other warriors, only with a more elaborate headdress. 'I am Queen Zyteea of the Usai tribe,' she says in a tongue you understand. 'What are you doing on this island?' You decide you have nothing to lose by telling Queen Zyteea the truth and so relate your story to her. If you have the word 'Sitnam' recorded on your *Adventure Sheet*, turn to **224**; otherwise, turn to **50**.

**114**

You slip down the slope and suffer cuts and bruises. Roll one dice and subtract the number rolled from your STAMINA score. If you roll a 6 you also lose 1 SKILL point. Turn to **219**.

**115**

You soon leave the jungle, with its strange sounds and rank smells of rotting vegetation, and find the ground rising as you head into the foothills of the mountains. As the sun climbs higher in the sky so you climb higher into the mountains. If you have the word 'Depacse' on your *Adventure Sheet*, turn to **335**. If not, *Test your Luck*. If you are Lucky, turn to **283**. If you are Unlucky, turn to **335**.

### 116

Managing to control your fear and stay calm, you gaze in fascination at the apparition materialising before you. The ghost looks like the woman carved as the figurehead for the ship. 'Help usss...' wails the ghost. 'The captain must be bested if we are to be freed. Help usss...' And then she is gone. Puzzled, you leave the room and:

| | |
|---|---|
| Open the other door? | Turn to 353 |
| Leave the ship? | Turn to 72 |
| Descend to the hold? | Turn to 26 |

### 117

Searching through the wreckage of the devastated buildings, you find nothing that has not been broken or destroyed. The curious thing is that there are no bodies among the destruction and no sign of the villagers in the surrounding jungle. Puzzled, you set off again south. Turn to 197.

### 118

(Deduct another 2 Gold Pieces from your total.) This time you are positive you have the right card – but when Armarno turns it over, it is black again! He has to be deceiving you! Now will you challenge the fraudster (turn to 258), leave his table (turn to 223) or leave the Gambling Pits (turn to 207)?

### 119

Just outside the city walls lies the cemetery. Its pillared entrance is decorated with disturbing statues and the fog merely adds to the eerie atmosphere of the place. Creeping between the weathered tombstones and mausoleums, you suddenly hear the crack of a twig somewhere off to your left and almost jump out of your skin. Spinning round, you are sure you catch a glimpse of something disappearing behind a grim sepulchre. You are not alone in the cemetery. Something else is also prowling around here during the hours of darkness. Peering round the corner of a crypt you see two men, who look like sailors, walking away from you through the mist, carrying a heavy-looking chest between them. Where can they be going? And what are they up to? If you have a Crab Doubloon, turn to **175**. If you do not, will you:

| | |
|---|---|
| Follow the two men to see where they go? | Turn to **312** |
| Launch a surprise attack on them? | Turn to **284** |
| Ignore them and leave the cemetery (add 1 Hour) to search elsewhere? | Turn to **52** |

### 120

Taking hold of the portcullis, you heave with all your might. Roll three dice and add 6 to the number rolled. If the total is less than or equal to your STAMINA score, turn to **99**. If it is greater, turn to **204**.

### 121

'That is correct. Congratulations,' says Calabrius, with a forced smile, and reluctantly hands you a bag containing 10 Gold Pieces. (Add these to your *Adventure Sheet* and regain 1 LUCK point.) With your confidence having been granted a boost, will you now look at the Arrow of Providence (turn to **81**), visit 'The Amazing Armarno' (turn to **9**) or leave the Gambling Pits (turn to **207**)?

## 122

Choose one of the items you are carrying and cross it off your *Adventure Sheet*. The creature eyes your gift with avid curiosity, turning it over and over in its hands. Fixing you with its glittering eyes it grins and says something in a twittering language you cannot understand. The capricious humanoid then disappears back into the jungle as abruptly as it first appeared, taking its treasure with it. You have just encountered a Rainforest Sprite and for giving it a gift you have received its blessing. (Restore 2 LUCK points.) Now turn to the paragraph with the same number as that which you noted down previously.

## 123

As soon as you touch the treasure you feel a tingling sensation in your fingertips. Looking down in horror, you see that your hands are turning to gold and you are no longer able to move them! There is nothing you can do as the transformation proceeds to affect your arms and soon your entire body. The next person to enter this chamber will marvel at the realism of the golden statue standing here.

### 124

Cinnabar lunges at you. Caught off guard you do not parry his thrust and, in shocked surprise, you feel the cold steel of his blade sink into your heart. You end your adventure and your life here, slain by the murderer of your family.

### 125

Once you are within the boundary of the jungle it is as if you have been transported into another world. A green twilight permeates everywhere under the canopy of the trees and you are surrounded by strange sounds and smells. An oppressive, prickly heat pervades the jungle, making the going harder than usual. Make a note of the number 385 on your *Adventure Sheet* and then turn to **192**.

### 126

Your opponents slump to the ground and you turn round to deal with the treacherous pirate. The old rogue is already fleeing as fast as he can along the alley. You run after him but, hearing your approach, the man spins round and lets fly a dagger. *Test your Skill.* If you succeed, turn to **173**. If you fail, turn to **213**.

### 127

You enter a small dark room and are immediately assailed by the heady smell of burning herbs. Through the smoke you make out a large man, sitting inside a chalk circle, wearing only a loincloth, macabre necklaces and a headdress of brightly coloured feathers. This must be Cinnabar's Witch-doctor, Malu. In one hand he holds a primitive wand, and the bodies of small, dead animals surround him. At your arrival, Malu snaps out of the trance-like state he was in and mutters something incomprehensible under his breath. Suddenly your head starts to spin. *Test your Skill*, adding 1 to the dice roll. If you succeed, turn to **44**. If you fail, turn to **87**.

### 128

The blazing ball drops towards the deck and, before you can get out of the way, smashes into your body. You double up in agony from the scorching. (Lose 5 STAMINA points.) Seeing a second such missile hurtling towards the ship, you take cover behind the mast. Turn to **232**.

### 129

Folklore has it that in the past pirates would kill one of their crewmen at the place where they buried their treasure or at a location they wanted kept secret, so that in death the ghost would guard it, unsleepingly. This is obviously what Cinnabar did here. Confidently, you speak the password: 'Crossbones.' Holding your breath, you await Jack A-Lantern's reaction.

'You may paasss...' hisses the pirate-ghost and sinks into the earth in front of you. Not waiting to be told twice, you hurry along the passageway, which ends in a flight of steps that descend under the cemetery. At the end of a short passageway you come to a

T-junction. Will you go left (turn to **221**) or right (turn to **13**)?

## 130

If you have a Magical Compass, turn to **172**. If not, will you threaten the castaway to make him tell you about the treasure (turn to **93**) or will you ignore him and explore the hills alone (turn to **65**)?

## 131

An undead sailor falls before you, felled by the mace of a tall figure, clad entirely in spiked armour. The silent Chaos Champion joined Cinnabar's crew to help him serve his dark masters better by spreading evil throughout all Ruddlestone.

CHAOS CHAMPION     SKILL 10     STAMINA 11

If you strike the warrior, roll one dice: on a roll of 1–3 your blow only causes the champion 1 STAMINA point of damage due to the protection of his armour. If the warrior strikes you, also roll one dice: on a roll of 5–6 his heavy mace causes you 3 STAMINA points of damage. If you defeat the Chaos Champion, turn to **298**.

## 132

Although you struggle valiantly to free yourself, ultimately you cannot. In minutes the tide raises the level of the seawater in the pit above your head and in a matter of a few more minutes, you have drowned. Your adventure ends here in a watery grave.

### 133

With a horrible squelching sound, the Chameleon's disgusting tongue, as long as its body, shoots out of its mouth and hits you. The sticky pad holds you fast as the Chameleon retracts its tongue, bringing you into its mouth. The monster bites down, injuring you severely (lose 4 STAMINA points and 1 SKILL point). If you are still alive, return to 53 and continue your battle.

### 134

The desk drawers are locked and, as there is no sign of a key, you try to force one. Eventually you manage to break open a drawer but at the same time trigger a blade that springs out of the desk into your wrist, cutting you badly (lose 2 STAMINA points and 1 SKILL point). Having staunched the bleeding, you go through the contents of the drawer. All you find are papers relating to the layout of Cinnabar's hideout in the Port of Crabs, which are of no use to you now. Will you now leave the room (turn to 233) or look at the globe (turn to 349), the chest (turn to 316) or the ship in a bottle (turn to 29)?

### 135

You turn on your heels and run! You hear a sharp crack behind you and then find yourself falling forwards as the Half-Ogre's whip wraps around your ankles and your feet are pulled from beneath you. (Lose 2 STAMINA points and 1 LUCK point, for being so cowardly!) In an instant the pirates are on you. Fight them both at the same time.

|  | SKILL | STAMINA |
|---|---|---|
| First PIRATE | 7 | 7 |
| Second PIRATE | 6 | 7 |

During the first Attack Round you are trying to get to your feet again, so you must reduce your Attack Strength by 2 points. If you win, turn to **187**.

### 136

Raising the whalebone effigy, you sense a thickening of the air around you and a dimming of the light, as if a cloud had crossed the face of the sun. In turn Quezkari seems to grow in stature. Your use of the Skeleton Artefact has aided his materialization on this Plane. (When you have to fight Quezkari, remember to add 1 point to his SKILL and 3 points to his STAMINA.) There is only just time to draw your sword before the unearthly spirit is upon you. Turn to **177**.

### 137

You hurriedly drag the Devotee's bodies to the side of the street before searching them. The two men have no possessions on them except for the sacrificial daggers. The hilts of these are made of ebony, carved to resemble human skulls, and on the backs of their right hands is the now so familiar image of a grinning black skull. The Devotees must have been out looking for victims to sacrifice to the bloodthirsty Quezkari – or maybe they were hunting you! But their presence could also indicate that the pirates' hidden base, or at least a temple to Quezkari, is close by. Will you continue your search here (turn to **396**) or now look

elsewhere to avoid meeting any more Devotees (turn to 52)?

## 138

You are not fast enough. Your spear-punctured body will remain as a grim warning to all those who would seek the cursed treasure of Blackscar.

## 139

As you draw your sword against Ramatu, he prepares to retaliate by casting a spell.

RAMATU                         SKILL 11         STAMINA 11

Consult the table below each time the High Priest wins an Attack Round to see which attack he uses and the damage it causes.

*Attack Round*  *Attack and Damage*

1st             Magical Darts: roll one dice and lose
                that many STAMINA points.

2nd             Quezkari's Curse: lose 1 SKILL point,
                1 LUCK point and 3 STAMINA points.

3rd             Bloodfire: Ramatu blasts you with jets
                of flaming blood, lose 4 STAMINA
                points.

4th onwards     Screaming Dagger: lose 2 STAMINA
                points and reduce your Attack
                Strength by 1 point for the rest of the
                battle due to the dagger's off-putting
                shrieks.

If you defeat the High Priest, turn to 7.

## 140

It is backbreaking work but after twenty minutes you have managed to clear a sizeable pile of stones from the cave-in, creating an opening into the tunnel beyond. It is only as you are partially through the hole you have cleared that the unstable tunnel roof gives way once more, crushing you under several tonnes of rock and earth. Your adventure ends here.

## 141

Opening the door and stepping through it, you find yourself in an obsessively tidy and disturbing room. The place looks like a laboratory. On the walls are detailed drawings of human and animal anatomy. Several shelves are packed with glass jars containing preserved body parts and even a human brain. A leather-bound journal resting on a desk is embossed in gold leaf with the name 'Doctor Malefact', the ship's surgeon and Cinnabar's notorious torturer. Do you want to search the Doctor's laboratory further (turn to **313**) or would you prefer not to linger here in case you are discovered (turn to **233**)?

## 142

You are accepted as a fellow warrior by the Usai and as a sign of this are given a Wristband of White Feathers, as worn by the other warriors of the tribe (regain 1 LUCK point). Queen Zyteea invites you to stay in the village that evening to share in their feast and you happily accept. Marlin's log was totally wrong about the inhabitants of Bone Island. Rather than being cannibals they are actually peaceable, intelligent, civilised people. With the moon now high in the night's sky, you dine on exotic fruits and spit-roast gazelle (restore up to 4 STAMINA points). As you eat, Zyteea tells you that the Usai people live in fear of Ramatu, the High Priest of Quezkari who lives in a temple in the mountains. He sends dark voodoo spirits against the tribespeople, carrying off warriors to become his Zombie slaves. Suddenly there is a scream from a tribesman on guard at the edge of the village. Everyone rushes to see what the disturbance is. The guard is suspended in mid-air and struggling as if in the grasp of some great creature. For a moment you think you see the shadowy outline of whatever is attacking the man. It is only momentary but you get the impression of a horny hide, large tusks, clawed hands and hairy, hooved legs, as if the thing were an amalgam of several different wild animals. The near-invisible Spirit-Beast roars and you run at it with your weapon drawn. If you are using a bone sword, turn to **23**. If not, turn to **234**.

## 143

Ignoring the pirate, you leave the markets of the Port of Crabs. (Make a note of the word 'Etarip' on your *Adventure Sheet*.) If you have the word 'Dnalsi' written on your *Adventure Sheet*, turn to **17**. If you do not, turn to **334**.

## 144

You dodge the silk strand, throwing yourself out of the way at the last second. Having wasted its spit attack, the Scarachna drops down from the trees and advances on you, trying to bite you with its mandibles and sting you with its tail.

SCARACHNA        SKILL 11      STAMINA 12

If the Scarachna wins an Attack Round, roll one dice. If you roll a 6, turn to **380**. If you reduce the Scarachna's STAMINA to 7 points or less, turn immediately to **292**.

## 145

Inside a shattered casket you find a corked Bottle of Rum still intact. Drinking the rum will restore 4 STAMINA points. Now return to **300** and choose another option.

## 146

Leaving the city, unnoticed, by the Kakhabad Gate you make your way through the darkness to Mallan's Point. The moon shines down from a cloudless sky, illuminating the crumbling tower that was once the port's lighthouse in more prosperous and peaceful times. But the moon is not the only light visible. Close to the edge of the cliff beyond the ruin you can see a flickering light. If you want to investigate this light, turn to **184**. If you would rather approach the lighthouse, turn to **220**.

**147**

As you unsheathe your weapon the pirate's grinning corpse rises from the coffin. 'Well, well,' the dead man says in a cracked voice, 'it's been so long since I've had a drink, poor old Roger could die of thirst, so he could.' With fangs bared and talon-hands raised, the vampiric pirate advances towards you.

JOLLY ROGER　　　　　　SKILL 9　　　STAMINA 10

If you kill the undead pirate, record the word 'Eripmav' on your *Adventure Sheet* and turn to **319**.

## 148

*Test your Luck.* If you are Lucky, turn to **21**; if you are Unlucky, turn to **43**.

## 149

The tunnel ends at a semicircular room on the far side of which is an ornately carved stone door flanked by two Zombie-like creatures with strange tribal masks covering their faces. As soon as you enter the chamber, the mindless guards shamble towards you. Will you engage in combat (turn to **226**) or flee from here (turn to **329**)?

## 150

You visit many of the seediest drinking establishments in the city, including The Cat and Cockroach, Angar's Mutiny and the Barnacle Tavern. However, your enquiries and investigations attract the attentions of those whose interest you did not want to arouse. Having just left yet another smoky bar-room, you suddenly find yourself confronted by a group of pirates and black-robed devotees – all followers of Quezkari. They have been alerted to your mission by your endless enquiries. Realising the danger you are in from Cinnabar's cronies, you run for it, as there are far too many for you to fight by yourself. *Test your*

*Luck.* If you are Lucky, turn to **241**. If you are Unlucky, turn to **33**.

### 151

Continuing along the passageway, eventually you reach the entrance to a vast, well-lit chamber. At one end of the cavern a man, dressed in black, flowing robes and with a headdress of crow's feathers, is chanting a spell over the corpse of a tribesman lying on a large, stone slab. Surrounding the Voodoo Priest and filling much of the chamber is a horde of Mask Zombies. Fascinated, you watch as the tribesman's corpse becomes pallid and withers. The Priest then places a tribal mask, which glows with an eldritch light, on its head and instantly the Zombie sits up. Then the Priest looks up, directly at you! With a screeching cry he points in your direction and his undead servants shamble forwards. There is only one exit from the chamber not blocked by the Zombies so will you run for it (turn to **201**) or stand and fight (turn to **45**)?

### 152

Cinnabar slumps to the deck: you have overcome him at last. But what is this? His wounds closing before your very eyes, Cinnabar rises to his feet again, seemingly unharmed! 'Don't you understand?' he mocks. 'The ceremony was completed. I am invulnerable and I shall be invincible! And do you know why?' Cinnabar is boasting now: 'My heart is no longer inside my body!' If you have a Fetish, turn to **398**. If not, turn to **124**.

**153**

As the *Fortune* sails away from the *Sea Maiden*, you watch as the ghost ship fades into thin air and the green mist disperses on the wind. At the same time the sky brightens once more. Suddenly there is a cry from the crow's nest: 'Captain Conyn! Galleon off the starboard bow!'

All eyes look out to sea. There on the horizon, sailing away from you, is the unmistakable shape of Cinnabar's pirate ship, the *Virago* – and the *Fortune* is gaining on it! Your quarry is in reach at last. Without warning, the sea before your vessel becomes a boiling froth. Out of this turbulence rises a gargantuan, fish-like head, jaws open wide. The whale-like Behemoth blots out the sun as its mouth descends on the *Fortune*, teeth like stalactites bearing down on you. The scene on board the *Fortune* is one of utter panic. Desperately the crew is trying to steer the ship out of the way of the monster, which is big enough to swallow it whole! The great jaws crash down on the *Fortune*, closing around the hold, breaking masts and spars as if they were matchwood. You are thrown across the deck and into the churning sea. Roll three dice: if the total is greater than your STAMINA score, turn to **344**; if it less, turn to **300**.

**154**

Gulping down the sweet liquid, you begin to feel more dexterous and clear-headed. You've just drunk a Potion of Skill (restore your SKILL score to its *Initial* level). Turn back to **217** and choose another option.

## 155

You find yourself dragged before Cinnabar once again, only this time it is on the deck of the pirate-lord's ship. 'So you escaped from our little trap,' the undead captain says, calmly. 'Well it won't happen again. I think this time you deserve the attentions of the good Doctor Malefact. Doctor?'

At Cinnabar's invitation, a small, elderly man with a balding pate and thick-lensed spectacles steps towards you, scalpel raised and a wicked glint in his eyes. You don't want to imagine what he has planned for you! You must try to escape. *Test your Skill*. If you are successful, turn to **250**. If you fail, turn to **107**.

## 156

Pocketing your 2 Gold Pieces (deduct these from your *Adventure Sheet*) Mundi takes a leather-bound tome from a bookcase and quickly thumbs through it. 'Ah, yes. Here we are,' he says, stopping at a particular page. 'This is a copy of the legendary Captain Marlin's log from his exploring days with the *Prancing Porpoise*. On one of his many voyages recorded in this journal, he mentions, in passing, a tropical island inhabited by cannibals, which he named Bone Island. There is no map but he does say that it lies 370 leagues east of the Port of Crabs. That's all I can tell you, I'm afraid,' says the Dwarf. 'If you ever go there, maybe you could make a few sketches that I could use to draw up a map of the place myself.' Thanking Mundi Pelago for his help, you go on your way. Turn to **334**.

### 157

The trap sprung, poison darts fly out of holes in the walls hitting you. Roll one dice and add 2: this is the number of darts that hit you, each one causing 1 STAMINA point of damage. Intending to be more careful in future, you stagger onwards, feeling like a human pincushion. Turn to **48**.

### 158

You come to tied to a stone altar before a hideous, bony likeness of the voodoo death-god, Quezkari. You only just have time to take in the fact that you are in a large underground chamber packed with pirates and Devotees, before a black-robed priest plunges his sacrificial knife into your heart! Your very blood will be used to help bring your enemy back to life! Your adventure is over.

### 159

Like a great felled tree, the Anchor Man topples onto the jetty with a crash. (Make a note of the word 'Rohcna' on your *Adventure Sheet*.) A rapid search of his body uncovers 6 Gold Pieces and a grubby piece of old parchment. On it is written one word: 'Leviathan'. What can it mean? You continue your search for secret entrances a while longer but discover nothing, so you give up looking here. Add 1 Hour and turn to **52**.

### 160

Holding out your arm, you allow Madame Galbo to open a vein with a thin knife so that she can collect some of your blood in a crucible (lose 3 STAMINA points). Just as you feel that you are about to faint, you hear the old wisewoman tell you that she is finished. Coming round, you watch as Madame Galbo heats the blood over a small flame, together with another strange liquid that smells strongly of sulphur. Clouds of steam form in the air above you and then, within them, form wraith-like faces. The old woman now sits swaying gently from side to side, with her eyes closed. 'Spirits,' she intones, 'what does the future hold for the vengeance-seeker? Tell us!'

An unnerving whispering moan fills the air and the spirits Madame Galbo has summoned speak: 'The Isle of Bones... That is where they must go... The spell-weaver's books hold the key... The mask holds the power... The heart of the idol... The Spirit of Darkness comes...' And then the voices fade.

Madame Galbo looks strained after the summoning so, bidding her farewell, you leave the cottage. Turn to **239**.

## 161

Evading your blows the two tentacles seize you in their slippery coils. There is nothing you can do as you are dragged into the sea and under the water. Through the churning murk you see the Giant Octopus that has made this cave its home. It is pulling you towards its snapping, beaked mouth. In desperation you manage to free you sword-arm, although one of the creature's tentacles still has you in its tightening grip. You are going to have to fight for your life.

GIANT OCTOPUS     SKILL 9     STAMINA 10

As you are fighting the Octopus underwater you must reduce your Attack Strength by 1 point for the duration of this battle. If the battle lasts for more Attack Rounds than your current SKILL score, turn to **190** straight away. If you defeat the creature in the same number of Attack Rounds as your current SKILL or fewer, turn to **379**.

### 162

You throw one portion of your Provisions into a far corner of the room (cross 1 meal off your *Adventure Sheet*). The mutant cat pounces on them and begins to devour them greedily. However, as soon as you enter the room, with a roar the beast bounds towards you. You have no choice but to fight the monster.

NINE-TAILS     SKILL 10     STAMINA 10

The cat attacks by trying to slash you with its great claws and bite you with its huge fangs. However, if the monster hits you, roll one dice. On a roll of 5 or 6, it has hit you with its barbed tails instead: roll one dice and deduct the number rolled from your STAMINA score. You may *Test your Luck* to avoid this damage if you wish. Keep track of how much STAMINA you lose in this way. If you survive this battle, turn to **235**.

## 163

You hand over the money (deduct 10 Gold Pieces from your *Adventure Sheet*) and the soldiers part to let you through. As you go Snide adds, 'But remember, if you should pass my way again...' Without further hesitation you hurry on, barely suppressing your anger at such an insult. Turn to **287**.

## 164

You eventually settle down with your back to a tree and your sword at your side, just in case. You are woken in the middle of the night by a loud buzzing. Hovering above you are three, oval-shaped beetles, each one as big as your head, with large mandibles and shimmering emerald bodies. Being carnivorous, the insects attack.

|                  | SKILL | STAMINA |
|------------------|-------|---------|
| First JUNGLE BUG | 5     | 5       |
| Second JUNGLE BUG| 4     | 4       |
| Third JUNGLE BUG | 5     | 4       |

If you kill all the flying beetles, you manage to get back to sleep and at dawn are on your way again. If you have the word 'Noogal' written on your *Adventure Sheet*, turn to **327**. If not, turn to **115**.

### 165

Taken from the head of one of the race of little people known as Elvins, who dwell in the Shamutanti Hills of Kakhabad and worship the Trickster God Lord Logaan, this lock of hair will bring you good fortune. Whenever you are instructed to *Test your Luck* from now on, you may deduct 1 from the dice-roll. Return to **42**.

### 166

Back in the outer entrance chamber of the temple, choosing a way you haven't gone yet, will you pass through the left-hand arch (turn to **216**), the central arch (turn to **392**) or the right-hand arch (turn to **255**)?

### 167

The clink of coins in his pot makes the blind man turn his head in your direction. 'Welcome, fellow traveller on life's highway,' he says in cheerful greeting. 'Give me your hand and I will tell you what waits within that unknown isle – the future.' Somewhat uncertainly, you stretch out your hand to the seer, who, after groping the air, clasps it in a vice-like grip. 'Ahhh,' he breathes, 'a brave soul that fights for truth and justice. May Cheelah smile upon your endeavours. Let Luck and Chance guide you on your path. Farewell.' Is that all you get for 2 Gold Pieces? The Master of Destiny releases your hand and says no more. Will you now make an offering to the bearded guru (turn to **393**) or the mute fortune-teller (turn to **98**), or will you go on your way (add 1 Hour and turn to **334**)?

**168**

At around noon the next day the previously clear sky suddenly, and inexplicably, darkens. As the *Fortune* sails on under the leaden sky another ship comes into view off the port bow. It appears to be in a state of terrible disrepair and is surrounded by a pall of sickly, green mist. Conyn looks at the vessel through his telescope and his face becomes ashen. You ask him what is troubling him. 'It is the *Sea Maiden* – a ghost ship,' he explains. 'Folklore has it that its crew and captain are cursed to sail the twelve seas for all eternity. We should avoid it at all costs!' You are now curious about the *Sea Maiden*. If you want to try to persuade Conyn to approach the ghost ship, turn to **390**. If not, turn to **153**.

**169**

Sure enough, in one cell you find five, half-starved tribespeople, whom you release. Having thanked you profusely for freeing them, they return the favour by giving you any information they can that may help you. They know nothing about the Pirates of the Black Skull but do know the Mask Zombies' secret: the masks themselves imbue the Zombies with Quez-kari's power, and if removed the undead become severely weakened. Knowing this, if you ever find yourself in combat with Mask Zombies, rather than fighting them in the usual way, you can try to remove their tribal masks. To do this very specific task you will have to reduce your Attack Strength by 2 points but as soon as you win an Attack Round you grab the Zombie's mask and cast it aside; the Zombie loses

2 STAMINA points and 3 SKILL points. If you had not saved the tribespeople, their fate would have been to be turned into Mask Zombies too. The prisoners also overheard the temple's High Priest telling one of his acolytes about a code or something and used the phrase, 'Back two, forward two. Back two, forward two.' Regain 1 LUCK point for this knowledge and then turn to **57**.

### 170

The bracelet is made from leather embedded with the razor-sharp teeth of a shark, thirty-eight in all, which point outwards. It is an unusual item, which at the moment does not seem to exhibit any magical potential – but it may prove useful. Return to **42**.

### 171

At last you come upon a rusted iron ladder set into one wall of a tunnel, which leads up to a manhole cover. Clambering out into the street above, you take in great lungfuls of fresh sea-air, glad to be rid of the vile stench of the sewers. Add 1 Hour and turn to **52**.

**172**

You are suddenly reminded of the Talismonger's words about the Magical Compass you bought and take it out of your backpack. Looking at it, you see that the needle is pointing westwards. If you want to head in the direction the compass is pointing, turn to **110**. If you would rather just explore the hills, turn to **65**.

**173**

You duck just in time to avoid being hit by the dagger. You then close on the old pirate. Turn to **318**.

**174**

Turfed out into the street, feeling insulted and frustrated, you set off to look elsewhere. Add 1 Hour to your total, and the word 'Regnad' to your *Adventure Sheet*, and then turn to **334**.

**175**

You are attracted to something lying in the soil of a freshly dug grave, glinting in the moonlight. Bending down, you pick it up – it is another doubloon, also with two heads. Crivens had such a coin and was a member of Cinnabar's crew, and now you have two men carrying a chest full of them through a deserted cemetery at night! They must have something to do with the Pirates of the Black Skull. You decide to follow these smugglers. *Test your Luck*. If you are Lucky, turn to **247**. If you are Unlucky, turn to **284**.

## 176

Clambering onto the statue, you force your sword into an eye-socket. You are suddenly aware of a hissing sound and see that purple smoke is pouring out of the iguana's mouth. Being so close to it you cannot avoid your head being surrounded by the cloud of gas. You pass out and fall onto the chamber floor. Death soon follows.

## 177

What sort of weapon are you using? If it is made of bone and you know how to awaken the power within it, convert the letters in its name into numbers using the code A=1, B=2, C=3 up to Z=26, add the numbers together and then turn to that paragraph. If you do not know how to release the weapon's magical energies or you are not using a bone sword, turn to **345**.

## 178

Drinking the 'Infusion of Fate' has the same effect as downing a Potion of Fortune. (Add 1 to your *Initial* LUCK score and raise it to this new level.) Return to **217** and do something else.

## 179

Madame Galbo applies herb compresses to your wounds, which knit together and heal within a matter of minutes! (Restore your STAMINA and SKILL scores to their *Initial* levels and regain 2 LUCK points.) 'Now you must be on your way,' orders the old wisewoman. Turn to **239**.

## 180

Still shaking, you uncork the bottle of Antidote and take a swig (reduce the amount left by one tot). The tremors soon subside and the fever also passes, leaving you able to go on your way. Turn to **262**.

## 181

An eerie silence pervades the streets of the Temple Quarter, creating a disconcerting atmosphere. Creeping, cat-like, along the roads, you are suddenly surprised by two figures that step out of the shadows in front of you. Dressed in black habits, and with sacrificial daggers raised, the Devotees advance towards you. Drawing your sword, you prepare to do battle. Fight them both at the same time.

|               | SKILL | STAMINA |
| ------------- | ----- | ------- |
| First DEVOTEE | 6     | 6       |
| Second DEVOTEE| 7     | 6       |

If the battle lasts longer than ten Attack Rounds, turn at once to **264**. If not, and you win the battle, turn to **137**.

## 182

The evil Cinnabar draws a gleaming cutlass from its scabbard and with a roar engages you in combat. At the same time, the pirate-lord's mangy parrot flies from its perch on his shoulder. 'That's right, Jezebel,' laughs Cinnabar, 'go for the eyes!'

CINNABAR       SKILL 12     STAMINA 16

As you are being distracted by the parrot you must reduce your Attack Strength by 1 point for this battle. Also, each Attack Round roll one dice: if you roll a 5 or 6, Jezebel pecks you and scratches you with her claws (lose 1 additional STAMINA point). If you manage to defeat the murderer of your family, turn to **152**.

## 183

If you offer the primitive some food, turn to **222**. If you give it a Flask of Grog or a Bottle of Rum, turn to **268**. If you offer it something else, turn to **246**.

## 184

Creeping cautiously towards the cliff edge you see that the light is actually that from a lantern, held by a woman who is looking out to sea with her two companions, a man and a pug-faced Man-Orc. Following the direction of their gazes, you make out a stout ship sailing towards the treacherous, jagged rocks, which line this stretch of coast. The light is guiding the ship to its doom! These three must be Wreckers, felons who deliberately cause shipwrecks for their own gain, scavenging the booty washed up from the sunken vessels. You must stop them or another ship will fall prey to their cruel intentions! Fortunately, they are still unaware of your presence here. Running at the nearest scoundrel, sword drawn, you wound him before he has a chance to defend himself. Fight the Wreckers all together.

|  | SKILL | STAMINA |
|---|---|---|
| First WRECKER | 7 | 5 |
| Second WRECKER | 6 | 7 |
| Third WRECKER | 8 | 7 |

If you win, turn to **369**.

### 185
Passing through the sweet-scented cloud, you follow the passageway until you reach a wooden door in the right-hand wall, barred from the outside. Listening at the door you can hear a scratching and snuffling sound. Do you want to open the door (turn to **311**) or go on without hesitation (turn to **151**)?

### 186
Having jumped ship you are now stranded in the middle of the Western Ocean with no sight of land anywhere. The turquoise waters stretch in every direction as far as the horizon. If you have the word 'Enutrof' recorded on your *Adventure Sheet*, turn to **257**. If not, turn to **54**.

### 187

Dropping his whip, the Half-Ogre moves in to attack you with his club.

HALF-OGRE SKILL 8 STAMINA 9

If the Half-Ogre wins an Attack Round, roll one dice. On a roll of 6, the blow from his club knocks you off your feet. This means that you spend the next round of combat getting up again, so you must reduce your Attack Strength by 2 points for that Attack Round. If you kill the Half-Ogre, turn to **328**.

### 188

You rush out of the temple into blazing sunshine. If you can catch up with Cinnabar maybe you'll be able to stop him before he leaves Bone Island. Running as fast as you can, you hurry down through the hills to the lagoon. Lose 1 STAMINA point due to this strenuous exercise. You reach the bay as evening approaches, just in time to see the *Virago* disappearing towards the horizon on the open sea. After all your efforts you are too late! If you have the word 'Nediam' written down on your *Adventure Sheet*, turn to **352**. If not, turn to **263**.

### 189

Raising the splintered shaft of wood in one hand you are amazed when the undead pirate cowers back hissing in fear. You quickly press home your advantage and plunge the stake into the corpse's chest, transfixing the creature's heart. Add 1 LUCK point and turn to **319**.

## 190

As you struggle valiantly against the Giant Octopus beneath the waves, eventually the air in your lungs runs out. Still submerged beneath the surface you gasp for breath, inhaling great lungfuls of salty brine. Whether you die by drowning or are devoured by the Octopus first, the end result is the same. Your adventure is over.

## 191

You step through the doorway into the watery light of dawn: you are on the deck of the *Virago*. Milling about in front of you are the crew and standing at the fo'c'sle is Cinnabar himself, a mangy parrot perched on his shoulder. Suddenly the evil captain looks round and, seeing you, screams to his pirates to capture you. There are far too many of them to take on by yourself so you do the only thing you can: you have no choice but to jump ship. The way to the side of the ship is blocked by the ruffians so you run for the rigging. Three pirates immediately step into your path.

|  | SKILL |
|---|---|
| First PIRATE | 6 |
| Second PIRATE | 5 |
| Third PIRATE | 7 |

Do not fight the Pirates in the usual way. Instead, calculate Attack Strengths for yourself and the first

Pirate. If his is higher, you are captured, turn to **155**. If yours is, you have barged past him: move on to the next Pirate and repeat the process until you have either been captured (turn to **155**) or evaded all three of the rogues ranged against you (turn to **79**).

### 192

Yammering cries, the shrieks of strange birds and the chittering of insects fill the jungle with a constant cacophony. But what was that? Something else is close by. Roll two dice. If you roll:

| | |
|---|---|
| 2 | Turn to **53** |
| 3 | Turn to **371** |
| 4 | Turn to **320** |
| 5 | Turn to **2** |
| 6 | Turn to **245** |
| 7 | Turn to **332** |
| 8 | Turn to **37** |
| 9 | Turn to **85** |
| 10 | Turn to **198** |
| 11 or 12 | No encounter |

Each encounter, apart from number 11 or 12, can occur only once. If you roll an encounter that has already taken place, roll again. If you roll 11 or 12, turn to the paragraph with the number you noted down before coming here. Ensure that you cross off each encounter as you choose it.

### 193

As you are trudging through the sludge and septic muck of the tunnels, a huge serpentine creature bursts from the foul water in front of you. The Sewer Snake must be almost five metres long, and is coloured a disgusting grey-brown. It attacks immediately.

SEWER SNAKE          SKILL 6          STAMINA 7

If you win, you go on until you eventually find a way out of the sewers. Add 2 Hours and turn to **52**.

### 194

'You have done very well,' says the tribespeople's Queen, 'but you have not done well enough to prove to us that your intentions are honourable. You must leave our village.' Before you go, however, Zyteea does tell you that her warriors have seen a ship anchored in the lagoon on the eastern side of the island. (Add the word 'Noogal' to your *Adventure Sheet*.) Leaving the village you head off into the jungle once more (turn to **164**).

### 195

'That'll do nicely,' smarms the guard, pocketing your gold and opening the gate. 'This way,' he says, leading you into the Old Fort. You soon find yourself outside a grand set of double doors. The guard knocks on the doors and having received the reply, 'Enter!' he opens them, letting you pass into Governor Montargo's audience chamber. Sitting behind a large oak desk, in a high-backed chair, is a dignified but bored-looking man, with close-cropped grey hair and wearing the uniform of a military commander. 'Well?' he demands, impatiently.

'Lord Montargo,' you begin, 'I am here to inform you of a terrible threat to the security of your city. The Pirates of the Black Skull are intending to return their evil captain, Cinnabar, to life through the dark practices of voodoo.'

'What nonsense! Cinnabar was killed six months ago by Conyn, the bounty hunter. The scoundrel's body was lost to the sea. How do you seriously expect me to believe that he can now be brought back to life?'

'I am telling you the truth!' you exclaim. 'I have seen evidence of the pirates' activities myself. We must find out where they are hiding. Do you want the Port of Crabs to become threatened by Cinnabar and those like him?'

'Enough! I am not interested in your wild goose chases and I do not have to listen to your paranoid ramblings. There is no threat to the city. Guards!' Four uniformed soldiers immediately burst into the audience chamber. 'My guest is just leaving.' The guards go to frog-march you away. Will you resist them (turn to 236) or allow yourself to be escorted out of the chamber (turn to 174)?

## 196

The spears just miss your back as you hurl yourself forwards. Picking yourself up from the tunnel floor, you reassess the situation. This place is proving to be more dangerous by the minute. Do you want to continue (turn to 228) or turn back and leave the caves (turn to 279)?

### 197

The trees soon begin to thin and in no time at all you find yourself at the edge of an expanse of marshland. The swamp is formed by a river delta where it meets the sea. As it is the only way onwards, you set off across it, wary of predatory swamp creatures. The going is quite easy through the marsh and, as dusk falls, you have almost reached dry land again. With the ground underfoot becoming firmer with every step you hear a loud buzzing getting closer too. And then the huge insect is there in front of you, its proboscis glistening with poison as it jabs at you. You must fight the Giant Mosquito.

GIANT MOSQUITO     SKILL 7     STAMINA 6

If you defeat the insect and lost *any* Attack Rounds to it, turn at once to **299**. If you managed to suffer no wounds in the fight, regain 1 LUCK point and turn to **262**.

### 198

You step through clinging fronds into a clearing in which a titanic struggle is taking place. There, in front of you, two colossi of the sweltering jungle – a huge grey-furred ape and a vicious, carnivorous lizard – are fighting over disputed territory. The Great Ape's fists are pounding the Terrible Lizard's scaly hide whilst the saurus snaps at the ape with its deadly jaws. Suddenly caught in the thick of things, what will you do?

| | |
|---|---|
| Side with the ape against the lizard? | Turn to **215** |
| Join in battle against the ape? | Turn to **337** |
| Try to skirt past the two monsters without getting involved? | Turn to **304** |
| Watch the fight to its conclusion? | Turn to **77** |

### 199

You also uncover a peculiar, eight-sided Blue Gem in a silk-lined box (add this to your *Adventure Sheet*). Having completed your search, you decide that it is time to find out what is going on here and so head in the other direction past the T-junction. Add 1 Hour to your total and turn to **13**.

### 200

If you bought the Ivory Lion Charm, turn to **227**. If not, you can either look for more practical equipment around the markets (turn to **351**) or leave to continue your quest (turn to **111**).

### 201

Evading the grasping hands of the Zombies you rush past them and along the new tunnel. Your heart racing with adrenalin, you skid to a halt on entering another cave. The Zombies are quite a way behind you now, but there is something far worse ahead. A fissure in the cave roof is open to the outside world and much of the chamber is a tangle of sticky webs. Crawling down from the crack on the glistening threads is a creature you had hoped never to meet again – the Scarachna! Since last you encountered the hybrid, the spider-scorpion has regained its strength and this time it is determined not to let you get away.

SCARACHNA        SKILL 11        STAMINA 12

If the monster wins an Attack Round, roll one dice. On a roll of 6, turn to **112**. If you ever lose two Attack Rounds in succession, turn to **336**. If you are still fighting after twelve Attack Rounds, turn to **237**. If you have killed the spider-scorpion within twelve Attack Rounds, turn to **30**.

### 202

You are inside a room full of nautical instruments and old charts. With a bang, the door slams shut behind you. You watch, terrified, as sextants and other objects rise into the air and the ship's compass in the room goes haywire. Then the wailing begins... *Test your Skill*. If you succeed, turn to **116**. If you fail, turn to **76**.

### 203

Hissing menacingly, the snakes slither towards you. Fight them as if they were a single opponent.

SNAKES        SKILL 8        STAMINA 11

The snakes have venomous bites and, if you lose an Attack Round, will cause 4 STAMINA points of damage (unless you have some Poison Antidote: taking one tot will keep the damage at 2 points). If you win, turn to **331**.

## 204

You cannot move the heavy, iron gate. If you are still able to use a Potion of Giant-Strength, turn to 31. If not, turn to 243.

## 205

With one of the jungle monsters dead, you are going to have to fight the other as it prepares to defend its territory once again. If the Great Ape won, turn to 330 to fight it, deducting any STAMINA points it lost in its battle with the saurus. If the Terrible Lizard won, turn to 278, deducting any STAMINA points it lost in its battle with the ape.

## 206

'You were warned, stranger,' the warrior intones and two of them immediately attack. Fight them simultaneously.

|                  | SKILL | STAMINA |
|------------------|-------|---------|
| First TRIBESMAN  | 8     | 7       |
| Second TRIBESMAN | 8     | 8       |

If you kill the warriors, the enraged villagers prepare to exact their revenge. If you hang around here you are sure to be killed so you flee, losing them in the jungle. Turn to 164.

## 207

Pushing through the bustling hordes of gamblers, you suddenly feel something pushed into your hand. Quickly looking about you, you think you see an old woman hurrying away but she is soon lost in the crowds. You have been given a sealed envelope. You wait until you are outside before breaking the wax-seal and opening the envelope. Inside are a letter and an iron key. The letter reads as follows:

*If you are determined to defeat the Pirates of the Black Skull, go to room 101 at the Silent Donkey.*
*A Friend.*

The key must be the one to the room in the inn. If you ever want to follow up this contact, turn to the paragraph with the same number as the room, but for now add 2 Hours to your total and turn to **334**.

### 208

You have no success in your search so you decide that your best option is to head northeast back into the island's interior. Turn to **279**.

### 209

Leaving the Grand Temple, you prepare to go on your way. During the day, the Street of Holies is packed with beggars, supplicants and worshippers. As you descend the temple steps, you hear two voices raised above the noise of the bustling crowds. One is shouting, 'Words of Wisdom! Words of Wisdom!' while the second is calling out, 'Let the Master of Destiny guide you on life's journey!' Looking round, you see three men sitting cross-legged beside the road. Each is dressed differently, in the manner of certain religious groups, but in front of each of them is a small offering pot. The closest of the men, with long hair and an even longer beard, smiles at you and says, 'Two Gold

Pieces is all we ask, and then we will reveal to you the mysteries of the cosmos and what Fate has in store for you.' Do you want to make a donation to one of the wise men (turn to **270**) or will you leave the Temple Quarter to look elsewhere for information (add 1 Hour and turn to **334**)?

Taking the fetish in your hands does not produce any ill effects so, thinking it could be useful later, you stow the grim little idol in your backpack. Will you now grab the pearl (turn to **388**) or leave the temple without further delay (turn to **188**)?

Descending the stairs you are enticed onwards by the smells of cooking. Entering a large, warm room in the hold, you find yourself in the pirates' kitchen and the cook doesn't appear too pleased at being interrupted. Bladderwrack the Cook is a huge, blubbery man, stripped to the waist and sweating disgustingly. Although his recipes for the crew are conventional fare, it is known that his own tastes are more cannibalistic, and a necklace of finger bones attests to this fact. Seeing that you are not one of the pirates, Bladderwrack picks up a pan of boiling water and hurls it at you. *Test your Skill*. If you succeed, turn to **35**. If you fail, turn to **339**.

## 212

The corpse pirate lets out a gurgling laugh as you wave the powerless wand at it. The undead horror lashes out at you with its ragged fingernails, clawing your face. (Lose 2 STAMINA points.) Turn to 147.

## 213

The dagger sinks into your shoulder. Lose 2 STAMINA points and turn to 318.

## 214

The mass of fighting bodies parts and there stands your quarry before you. Having fought your way past his lackeys, you are face-to-face with Cinnabar, old Bloodbones himself, at last. But he is no longer the undead horror you encountered beneath the Port of Crabs – he is now the debonair, handsome pirate-lord he was before his death. Springing like a panther, you sprint across the deck to reach Cinnabar. At the same time the pirate captain raises a small crossbow and fires. *Test your Skill*. If you succeed, turn to 375. If you fail, turn to 102.

## 215

With you joining the fight against the Terrible Lizard, the Great Ape soon prevails. With one last blow from the ape's huge fists, the saurus falls to the ground either dead, or unconscious. The ape fixes you with its beady black eyes. Rearing up on its haunches it bellows and begins beating its chest. Will you prepare to defend yourself (turn to 330), or will you run for it (94)?

**216**

You have not travelled very far along the passageway beyond the left-hand archway when the corridor turns left into a small, dark, rough-hewn chamber. Curiously, pieces of shipping tackle seem to have been abandoned here, including a ship's wheel, but the object which intrigues you most lies in the middle of the floor. It is a plain wooden coffin, draped with a Jolly Roger. There is no way out of the chamber other than the way you came in, so will you:

| | |
|---|---|
| Search the chamber for any useful items? | Turn to **314** |
| Open the flag-draped coffin? | Turn to **36** |
| Retrace your steps and pass through the central archway? | Turn to **392** |
| Go back and choose the right-hand archway? | Turn to **255** |

**217**

The box contains several empty bottles, no doubt drunk by Balinac. However, there are two with their seals still intact that are labelled. Do you want to:

| | |
|---|---|
| Drink the 'Essence of Expertise'? | Turn to **154** |
| Drink the 'Infusion of Fate'? | Turn to **178** |
| Study the *Mythica*? | Turn to **47** |
| Read the *Arcanum*? | Turn to **5** |
| Leave the wizard's cell? | Turn to **385** |

## 218

With your fingers round the handle of the door, you freeze, hearing a floorboard creak outside the room. Is there somebody there – somebody up to no good? Silently, you unsheathe your sword, just in case, and open the door but do not step through it. Instantly, two black-robed figures leap into the doorway, coshes raised. Determined to stop you succeeding in your quest, the Devotees of Quezkari attack. In the narrow doorway you can fight these acolytes of evil one at a time.

|  | SKILL | STAMINA |
|---|---|---|
| First DEVOTEE | 6 | 7 |
| Second DEVOTEE | 6 | 6 |

If you win, a rapid search of the fanatics' bodies reveals nothing of value to you so you quickly leave the inn. Add 1 Hour and the word 'Yeknod' to your *Adventure Sheet*, then turn to **287**.

## 219

Reaching the edge of the cave you can now see that a narrow ledge, just a few metres above the crashing waves, leads into the gloomy depths beyond. Do you want to continue into the cave (turn to **354**) or would you rather give up on this course of action and return to the cliff-top (turn to **322**).

### 220

To your surprise, you find a sturdy door in the base of the tower, the only way in. Being as quiet as possible, you try the door but discover that it is locked. What will you do now?

| | |
|---|---|
| Attempt to break down the door? | Turn to **326** |
| Investigate the flickering light? | Turn to **184** |
| Leave the lighthouse (add 1 Hour) and look elsewhere for the pirates? | Turn to **52** |

### 221

You find yourself exploring the pirates' hideout, a collection of meeting rooms, storerooms and sleeping chambers, but all appear to be deserted! Do you want to remain here and make a thorough search of the hideout (turn to **305**) or would you rather return to the T-junction and follow the tunnel in the opposite direction (turn to **13**)?

### 222

The Balinac snatches the food from you and wolfs it down (cross off 1 meal from your Provisions), allowing you to pass. Turn to **125**.

### 223

Will you now look at the Arrow of Providence (turn to **81**) or Calabrius's Calculator (turn to **294**), or leave the Gambling Pits (turn to **207**)?

### 224

While you are recounting recent events, a tribesman approaches Zyteea and you recognise him as the one you saved from the Praying Mantis. He whispers something to his Queen and when you are finished she says, 'Toombei tells me that you saved his life and that you are a noble warrior. Therefore you are welcome here.' Turn to **142**

### 225

As you rummage about inside the dead pirate's coffin, you disturb a number of Blood Maggots that were lurking there. Each of the eyeless grubs latches onto your flesh with its barbed mouthparts. Roll one dice. This is how many of the maggots bite you. Lose the same number of STAMINA points. Having managed to pull the horrid creatures from your ravaged flesh, you hastily depart the vampire's chamber. You have no desire to remain there any longer. If you have the word 'Eripmav' written on your *Adventure Sheet*, turn to **58**. If not, turn to **166**.

### 226

Armed with pole-arms, the Mask Zombies are dangerous enemies.

|  | SKILL | STAMINA |
|---|---|---|
| First MASK ZOMBIE | 8 | 7 |
| Second MASK ZOMBIE | 8 | 6 |

If you overcome your adversaries, turn to **291**.

## 227

'If you're worried about voodoo, you should go and see Madame Galbo,' says the Talismonger and tells you how to find her cottage in Mandrake's Lane. If, in future, you are given a chance to visit Madame Galbo, you may do so by turning to **100** (make a note of this paragraph number on your *Adventure Sheet*). But for now, you can either look for more practical equipment around the markets (turn to **351**) or leave to continue your quest (turn to **111**).

## 228

Not much further on, the tunnel comes to an end before a blank rock wall at the foot of which is a murky pool. There is no sign of any treasure and there appears to be no way on... unless it's through the pool! But then you don't know how deep the pool is or for how long you may have to hold your breath. Will you dive into the water (turn to **71**) or now turn back (turn to **279**)?

## 229

Leaping between the man and the Mantis you ready your sword. Its forelegs raised ready to strike and snapping its mandibles, the monstrous insect attacks.

GIANT PRAYING
MANTIS                SKILL 7        STAMINA 7

The Mantis is covered in armour-like chitin so blows against it will only inflict 1 point of damage (2 points if you use LUCK in this battle and are Lucky, but no points if you are Unlucky). If you win, turn to **368**.

### 230

*Crump!* The heavy iron anchor hits you in the side, the force of the blow knocking you to the floor. Lose 3 STAMINA points. Looking into the fog you can make out a shadowy figure advancing towards you. Desperately, you try to unsheathe your weapon. Turn to **231**.

### 231

The swathes of mist part and a tall, barrel-chested man, built like an ox and with muscles like ship's cables, stands before you. In his hands he holds a heavy iron chain on the end of which swings the anchor. 'Stranger, let me introduce myself. I'm the Anchor Man,' growls the pirate assassin, 'and now it's time to die.' As the thug prepares to use the anchor against you like a morning-star, you spot the black skull tattooed on the back of his right hand.

ANCHOR MAN      SKILL 9      STAMINA 10

Every time the Anchor Man strikes you, roll one dice: on a roll of 5–6, the anchor causes you 3 STAMINA points of damage rather than the usual 2. If you are lying on the floor, if you win the first Attack Round you do not injure the pirate (do not deduct any STAMINA points) but you manage to unsheathe your sword and fend off the assassin, so giving you time to get to your feet. From then onwards, you can fight as normal. If you win two consecutive Attack Rounds against the Anchor Man, turn at once to **271**. If he wins two consecutive Attack Rounds, turn to **105**. If you defeat the assassin, turn to **159**.

## 232

The fireball crashes into the deck, smashing a hole in the rotten planks, but still the phantom vessel skims onwards over the sea. The *Virago* cannot out-run Velyarde's craft and before the pirates really know what is going on, the undead crew of the *Sea Maiden*, followed by yourself, are boarding the galleon. Battle immediately ensues as the undead sailors avenge themselves on Cinnabar's cronies. Roll one dice. If you roll 1–2, turn to **15**; 3–4, turn to **131**; 5–6, turn to **298**.

## 233

Choosing somewhere you haven't already been, will you:

| | |
|---|---|
| Descend the staircase? | Turn to **211** |
| Open the far door? | Turn to **191** |
| Open the door marked 'Captain'? | Turn to **97** |
| Open the door to the right? | Turn to **141** |
| Open the door to the left? | Turn to **127** |

## 234

Although you attack valiantly, your weapon proves ineffective against the conjured horror. With one sweep of a tiger-like paw, the Spirit-Beast hurls you into the side of a hut, cracking several of your ribs. (Lose 5 STAMINA points and 1 SKILL point.) Dropping the body of the dead tribesman, the thing goes on a rampage, crushing buildings and killing villagers that are in its path. Eventually the Usai manage to drive the Spirit away, thanks to the spells of the tribe's shaman, but not before it has devastated their village. When morning comes there is much relief all round. Disheartened that you were unable to help Queen Zyteea and her people you set off for the Temple of Quezkari in the mountains (lose 2 LUCK points and turn to **115**).

## 235

Exhausted after such a titanic struggle, you take a few minutes to recover from the fight. If you have some Poison Antidote and the beast stung you at all with its tails, you may recover half the STAMINA points lost in this way by drinking one tot. Now that you are no longer being threatened by a ravening monster, you take time to look around the room you are in. It is a spartan affair, containing just a few pieces of broken furniture, but on the other side of it is a door leading onwards. You also notice an entrance to a cave with the iron portcullis that barred it raised. Obviously the pirates let the Nine-Tails out into the main room to stop anyone from following them. The mutant itself was captured by Cinnabar on one of his voyages and brought back to the Port of Crabs to guard the entrance to his innermost sanctum. Do you want to open the door (turn to 323) or would you rather investigate the cat's cave first (turn to 69)?

## 236

Overcome by the guards, you soon find yourself languishing in a stinking prison cell. (Add 1 Hour to your total.) Eventually a stern-faced figure appears at the grille in the cell door. It is the head of the City Guard, Captain Snide. 'Enjoying your stay?' he says with a mocking sneer. 'Well let's say ten Gold Pieces and you can go on your way.' Will you pay the sadistic Captain the bribe, if you can afford to (turn to 254), or will you wait and attempt to get out by yourself when the coast is clear (turn to 19)?

## 237

With your battle against the Scarachna still raging, the Mask Zombies catch up with you. Three of them start to attack you while you are still fighting the spider-scorpion! You must now fight all four opponents at the same time.

|  | SKILL | STAMINA |
|---|---|---|
| First MASK ZOMBIE | 7 | 6 |
| Second MASK ZOMBIE | 8 | 6 |
| Third MASK ZOMBIE | 7 | 5 |

If you somehow manage to defeat all your opponents, turn to 30.

## 238

Conyn and his crew remain on board the *Fortune* as you leap across the gap between the two ships and onto the ill-fated *Sea Maiden*. It appears to be deserted so you decide to descend below decks to explore further. Creeping along an empty corridor, you hear a frantic squeaking and out of the gloom scampers a horde of ghostly rats, fangs gleaming and eyes glowing red – and you are directly in their way. Will you flee while you still have the chance (turn to **72**) or stand your ground (turn to **289**)?

## 239

Add 1 Hour to the time you have taken on your quest so far. Leaving Mandrake's Lane, you consider where to start looking for the pirates' hideout. Will it be:

The Temple Quarter?                    Turn to **181**
The Port of Crabs' inns and taverns?   Turn to **150**
The ruined lighthouse?                 Turn to **146**
The docks?                             Turn to **67**
The sewers under the city?             Turn to **355**
The cemetery?                          Turn to **83**

**240**

Losing your balance at the last moment, you fall headfirst into the ten-metre deep pit full of gleaming spear-length iron spikes. The traps inside the Temple of Quezkari were not designed to be survived.

**241**

Somehow, you manage to evade capture by running through the alleyways and backstreets of the port. (Add 1 Hour to your total.) If it is still daylight, turn to **334**. If night has already fallen, turn to **52**.

**242**

Along the shoreline you find several coconuts and a bunch of bananas, all in all enough food for 3 meals. Return to **300** and choose another option.

**243**

The portcullis had to be heavy to stop the Nine-Tails getting out so you have no hope of lifting it. Trapped in the cave, there is no way that you will be able to continue on your quest.

## 244

Picking up the skull, you are suddenly filled with an almost overpowering sense of fear and paranoia. You have suffered a terrible curse (lose 2 LUCK points and 1 SKILL point)! Involuntarily, you drop the skull, smashing it on the floor. Turn to **55**.

## 245

There is a movement in the bushes in front of you and a tall, flightless bird bursts into your path. The creature has an axe-shaped bill and, squawking, it attacks, trying to peck you, and kick you with its huge clawed feet.

AXEBILL        SKILL 9      STAMINA 13

If you kill the bird, wondering what other surprises the fauna of the island has in store, you set off again through the boiling jungle. Turn to the paragraph with the same number as the one you wrote down.

## 246

The creature grabs your gift and, having sniffed it, hurls it away into the sea (cross the object off your *Adventure Sheet*). It then proceeds to growl menacingly. Will you quickly offer it some food (turn to **222**), a Flask of Grog or Bottle of Rum (turn to **268**), or will you prepare to defend yourself (turn to **95**) or run for it into the jungle (turn to **125**)?

247

The smugglers eventually stop outside an old tomb over-grown with moss and ivy. Pushing open the granite door, they disappear inside. You wait a few minutes before lighting your lantern and passing through the portal yourself. (Add 1 Hour to your total.) Your lantern reveals a passageway leading away into the gloom. As soon as you step over the threshold, another light becomes visible at the other end of the corridor and starts to move towards you. Gliding along the passage is the apparition of an old man with sunken eye-sockets and talon-like fingernails clogged with grave-dirt. The sight of the glowing spectre fills you with a sense of dread and your blood runs cold when you see that the lantern it carries has been fashioned from a human skull. From the tales you have heard told of the Port of Crabs, you know that this must be the ghostly Jack A-Lantern. The ghost does not attack you but instead comes to a halt a few metres from you. Its jaw drops open and the apparition utters one word: 'Paasswoord...' Do you know a password? If so, now is the time to say it. Convert the letters of the password into numbers using the code A=1, B=2, C=3 and so on: then add up the numbers and turn to the paragraph, which is the same as the total. If you do not know a password or the paragraph you turn to makes no sense, turn to **269**.

## 248

Roll three dice, unless you have an Ivory Lion Charm, in which case just roll two. If the total rolled is less than or equal to your STAMINA score, turn to 82. If it is greater, turn to **62**.

## 249

The pressure in your lungs becomes unbearable and, before you can free yourself from the chain, you open your mouth. Freezing brine rushes into your air passages and you drown. The Anchor Man has succeeded. Your adventure is over.

## 250

Seizing the opportunity while your captors are distracted by Malefact, you twist free of their grasp and leap to your feet. The good Doctor and your two captors attack at once. Fight them all at the same time.

|  | SKILL | STAMINA |
|---|---|---|
| DOCTOR MALEFACT | 7 | 6 |
| GARBOIL | 6 | 8 |
| STRAKE | 7 | 7 |

If you win within 15 Attack Rounds, you make your break for freedom (turn to **79**). If not, you are surrounded and taken prisoner again (turn to **107**).

## 251

The spell animating it broken, the Golem collapses into a heap of gold and jewels. The bone weapon served you well in your fight with Blackscar's cursed hoard and its edge was not dulled by the Golem's hard body, so you decide to keep hold of it (note it down on your *Adventure Sheet*. Whenever you are in combat with Undead, spirits or magical creatures using this weapon, you may add 1 point to your Attack Strength.) With your new weapon, will you now leave the caves straight away (turn to **279**) or first take some of the treasure after all your efforts to find it (turn to **123**)?

### 252

While you are making your search you are bitten by a venomous Redback Spider (lose 3 STAMINA points). Having completed your search you decide that it is time to find out what is going on here and so head in the other direction past the T-junction. Add 1 Hour to your total and turn to **13**.

### 253

Leaving the room you come face-to-face with three of the *Virago's* crew in the corridor. In the confines of the passage you are grabbed and dragged through the far door. Turn to **155**.

## 254

You hand over the money through the grille (deduct the 10 Gold Pieces from your *Adventure Sheet*) and with a clattering of bolts, Snide unlocks the cell door. As you go, the corrupt Captain calls out to you, 'But remember, if you should cross my path again...' Turn to **287**.

## 255

Passing under the archway, you find yourself following another tunnel even deeper into the mountain. Then there is a click as your foot touches a fixed stone and for a split second you wonder if you have made a mistake. Reacting instantly, you throw yourself forward to avoid the trap. *Test your Luck*. If you are Lucky, turn to **86**. If you are Unlucky, turn to **157**.

## 256

The water does not come higher than your waist. You are half way across, in the midst of the stream, when the water begins to froth and boil. You feel the pinpricks of tiny, sharp teeth biting (lose 2 STAMINA points) and look down into the water to see that a shoal of Piranhas has decided to make you its next meal.

PIRANHAS            SKILL 6        STAMINA see below

To calculate the Piranhas' STAMINA score, roll one dice and add 6. This is the total number of the voracious fish attacking you. Each fish has 1 STAMINA point. If you defeat the frenzied feeders, you are able to finish crossing the river and climb out onto the opposite bank. Turn to the paragraph with the number you noted down previously.

## 257

Treading water, you catch sight of a vessel in the distance. Waving your arms furiously, you succeed in attracting the crew's attention. The sailors immediately set a course to pick you up. The ship comes alongside and you are hauled on board. Fortunately your oilskin backpack has kept all your Provisions and possessions safe and dry. You are greeted by a handsome man whose face is tanned from exposure to the elements and scarred on one side. 'Welcome to the *Fortune,*' he says. 'I am her captain and a bounty hunter by trade. My name is Conyn.' What, Conyn the bounty hunter – the man who killed Cinnabar? 'The very same,' he admits proudly. 'But tell me, who are you and how come we find you alone in the middle of the ocean?'

You relate your tale to a credulous Conyn over some fine Femphreyan port in his quarters, and by the time your story is done his expression has lost its former cheeriness. 'Will you help me stop Cinnabar?' you ask.

'Of course I shall,' says Conyn, resolutely, 'but how are we to find him? Do you know where the *Virago* was headed?' If you do, you should have two coordinates. Subtract the easterly distance from the southerly one and turn to the paragraph with the same number as the result. If the paragraph you turn to makes no sense, or you have no idea where to go, there is nothing you can do to follow Cinnabar and so you cannot stop him. You have failed in your quest!

## 258

'You accuse me of *cheating*?' exclaims Armarno, incensed. 'I have never been so insulted in all my days. Just because *my* hand is faster than *your* eye!' Angered by the trickster's words, you jump to your feet and, in doing so, knock over the table. The three cards fall onto the floor – they are all black! Armarno must have palmed the white. You were right all along. Cursing the man, you prepare to unsheathe your sword but stop, feeling a strong hand on your shoulder. The gruff voice of a Troll growls in your ear: 'I said, no fighting.' Before you can stop them, the two Trolls snatch your sword from you and between them deposit you weaponless, and with your pride bruised, in the street outside. Without your sword, you will have to fight with your Attack Strength reduced by 3 points until you can get hold of another weapon. Disgruntled, you leave to search elsewhere (add 2 Hours and turn to **334**).

**259**

You cross the log safely and once you are on the other side the blindfold is removed and you are taken before Queen Zyteea again. 'You have passed the first part of your test,' she says. 'For the second and final part will you choose the Challenge of the Cat (turn to **34**) or the Challenge of the Shell (turn to **290**)?'

**260**

*Test your Luck*. If you are Lucky, turn to **109**. If you are Unlucky, will you move on to Calabrius's Calculator (turn to **294**), visit 'The Amazing Armarno' (turn to **9**), or leave the Gambling Pits (turn to **207**)?

**261**

Madame Galbo takes three substances from some of the jars in front of her on the table and mixes them together in her mortar. 'Wraith Grass seeds, powdered human bones, and dried Basilisk's blood combine to make a potent defence against those unfortunates resurrected from their graves to walk the world as Zombies.' The old wisewoman gives you the resulting powdery compound in a stoppered gourd. Madame Galbo explains that there is enough Zombie Dust for four uses. You may use the powder once for each encounter you have with Zombies. Each time you use it, one of these undead creatures will be repelled so you can treat the outcome as if you had killed it. Make a note of this on your *Adventure Sheet* and then turn to **239**.

### 262

Safely out of the marsh at last, you settle down to sleep under the stars. After your encounter with the mosquito the night passes peacefully and you wake the next day feeling refreshed. (Regain 2 STAMINA points.) Keen to find the pirates, you set off again at a brisk pace and soon enter a range of low, scrub-covered hills. Progressing further, you hear laughter coming from behind one outcrop. Climbing to the top you look down and are surprised to see a roughly made shelter. Dancing around in front of it, chuckling to himself, is a skinny old man with a long, straggly white beard and large straw hat. His clothes are tattered and torn and he looks like he might originally have come from the Old World. Looking up he sees you and calls out, 'Ho, stranger! Lovely weather for the time of year.' The man then bursts out laughing again: he is obviously totally mad! 'You'll be looking for Blackscar's treasure then.' What is the old lunatic whittering on about? Do you want to press him about the treasure (turn to **360**), talk to him, hoping to find out more about the island and its inhabitants (turn to **381**), or leave the insane castaway and explore the hills (turn to **65**)?

### 263

You fall to your knees on the sand with your head in your hands. Stranded on Bone Island there is nothing you can do to stop Cinnabar returning to the Port of Crabs and succeeding with his wicked scheme.

### 264

As you are fighting, several other Devotees round a corner and it is not long before you are restrained. There is a sudden, sharp blow to the back of your head and you blackout... Turn to 158.

### 265

As the last Zombie slumps to the floor, you hear a voice calling for help in a strange tongue, but one that you understand, from one of the cells. Do you want to help whoever is imprisoned here (turn to 169) or would you rather not waste any more time here and continue your search of the temple to find Cinnabar (turn to 57)?

### 266

You turn round and come face-to-face with two black-robed figures, their faces hidden by the hoods of their habits. Wielding heavy coshes, the Devotees advance on you. You will have to fight them both at the same time.

|               | SKILL | STAMINA |
|---------------|-------|---------|
| First DEVOTEE | 7     | 5       |
| Second DEVOTEE| 6     | 6       |

If you win, turn to 126.

### 267

In no time at all the *Fortune* is heading southeast across the Western Ocean. While on the voyage you rest and recover some of your strength. (Restore up to 4 STAMINA points.) After a day you are approaching the Crab Reefs. Conyn's helmsman skilfully directs the vessel through the treacherous waters and it looks like the *Fortune* is going to get through unscathed. Then at the last minute disaster strikes! There is a terrible grating sound as the *Fortune's* hull scrapes across something in the channel and comes to a halt. At the same time, several pairs of enormous pincers emerge from the sea. The ship is under attack from Giant Crabs. You attack the nearest of the huge crustaceans clambering up the vessel's side.

GIANT CRAB          SKILL 7      STAMINA 9

If you kill the Crab, turn to **370**.

## 268

The primitive grabs the container and gulps down its contents. A smile slowly curls its lips and the creature addresses you. 'Thank you,' it mutters. 'It is good wine. Master had good wine. Magical wine. Made Balinac see strange things and feel dizzy. Balinac take you to Master's cell. You come?' If you want to go with the primitive, turn to **24**. If not, you set off alone into the jungle (turn to **125**).

## 269

'Intruder!' screams the pirate-ghost and flies at you, shrieking. You draw your weapon but every time you strike the horror, your blade passes straight through it, whereas you feel the spectre's claws tearing at your flesh like cruel knives. There is no way you can defeat the ghost. An unpleasant death awaits you and your adventure is most definitely over.

## 270

You pause while you try to decide which of these wise men to consult. The long-haired man is wearing a loose-fitting orange robe and is seated on a board of long iron nails, with apparently no discomfort. The second seer, the self-proclaimed Master of Destiny, is bald and wears a grey robe covered with mystic symbols. You now also notice that he is blind. The last figure is swathed from head to toe in festering rags and in front of him sits a deck of cards. He says nothing. The only way you are going to get anything out of these characters is if you make them an offering of 2 Gold Pieces. Which will it be?

| | |
|---|---|
| The bearded guru? | Turn to **393** |
| The sightless seer? | Turn to **167** |
| The speechless fortune-teller? | Turn to **98** |

## 271

Under your relentless onslaught, the pirate stumbles backwards, getting his feet caught up in the heavy chain, and falls onto the hard, wooden planks, dropping the anchor. Quickly, seizing the opportunity, you give the anchor a shove, pushing it off the jetty and into the water. The anchor sinks rapidly, pulling the Anchor Man into the harbour. Unable to free himself from the tangled chain, the panicking pirate disappears from view under the dark waters, never to surface. (Make a note of the word 'Rohcna' on your *Adventure Sheet*.) You continue your search for secret entrances a while longer but find none, so you give up looking here. Add 1 Hour and turn to **52**.

## 272

The ledge crumbling away behind you, you race onwards as the crashing of rocks echoes through the cavern. Ahead of you a great crack appears across the path and before you even have a chance to leap over it, the entire section you are on gives way, plunging you to your death.

## 273

As you drop through the broken slats of the bridge you grab at the rough ropes that hold it all together. You manage to grab hold of a knotted cord halting your abrupt drop but jarring your shoulder. (Lose 1 STAMINA point.) You hang over the yawning gulf beneath you for a moment, recovering from the shock, before hauling yourself back up onto the bridge and cautiously continuing along the rest of the way. At last you step off the bridge, entering the cliff-face through the skull's open mouth. You find yourself in a high-ceilinged, torch-lit tunnel, which cuts its way deep into the mountain. It is not long before the tunnel opens out into a large, square chamber. Hideous painted carvings adorn the walls here but there is nothing else of interest in the room. However, three archways in the opposite wall lead onwards into the temple. Will you proceed through the archway to the left (turn to **216**), through the one in the centre (turn to **392**), or by passing under the archway to the right (turn to **255**)?

### 274

As you stroll boldly into the village you are immediately surrounded by several warriors. If you have a Darkwood Armband, turn to **56**. If not, turn to **113**.

### 275

The door opens and you step through into a large, circular room. At its centre is a magnificent sight: the biggest crystal you have ever seen stands on a plinth, glowing with an inner light. However, covering the floor around the plinth are countless writhing snakes, and despite the mystical beauty of the crystal, an incipient sense of evil permeates this place. You are sure the artefact has something to do with the power of Quezkari on the island. If you want to try to destroy the huge crystal, turn to **203**. If not, you will have to leave and return to the passage, turn to **329**.

### 276

Turning your back on the undead pirate was a bad idea. It is on you in a flash and sinks its unnaturally developed fangs into the bad of your neck (lose 2 STAMINA points). You have no choice now but to defend yourself with your sword. Turn to **147**.

## 277

The Usai are full of gratitude for you now that you have rid them of the High Priest's Spirit-Beast. Queen Zyteea explains that the evil wizard summoned it to destroy another village on the island and that it had also 'haunted' them for several nights. Looking at the bone weapon Zyteea says, 'I am sure that with Nightdeath in your hands you will be able to vanquish both Ramatu and Cinnabar. But to help you further I give you this Bolarang.' She hands you a peculiar looking wooden cross with struts of equal length that end in curved points. The Bolarang is used like a throwing dagger but always returns to its owner once thrown. Before a fight you may use this weapon against one opponent: *Test your Skill* and, if you succeed, reduce their STAMINA by 2 points. At dawn, with the tribespeople's praises ringing in your ears, you leave the village. Zyteea also told you that her warriors had seen a ship anchored in the lagoon to the southeast, so will you head in that direction (turn to **10**) or into the mountains to find the Temple of Quezkari (turn to **115**)?

## 278

No sooner than the ape is lying dead on the floor of the clearing, the Terrible Lizard turns on you with a primeval roar.

TERRIBLE LIZARD      SKILL 7      STAMINA 11

If you win, leaving the two corpses of the colossi behind you, you continue on your way. Turn to the paragraph with the number you noted down previously.

### 279

Leaving the hills behind you, you set off northeast-wards, towards the centre of the island again. Your route takes you through the easternmost part of the marsh once more, back in the direction of the dense jungle. Roll one dice. If you roll 1–4, make a note of the number 397 and turn to **192**. If you roll 5–6, turn to **359**.

### 280

The water inside the cave now begins to boil and from the turmoil rises a hideous grey-green monstrosity. Reaching for you with sucker-lined tentacles, the Giant Octopus intends to pull you into its snapping, beaked mouth and devour you. Once again you find yourself fighting for your life.

GIANT OCTOPUS          SKILL 9          STAMINA 10

If the Octopus ever scores two successful hits in succession, turn to **46**. If you kill it, turn to **73**.

### 281

Barrels and crates from the *Fortune* are among the items washed up among the driftwood, and could contain something of use to you. Roll one dice. If the number you roll is odd, turn to **387**; if it is even, turn to **145**.

### 282

You turn the corner and find the old man standing in front of you. 'So nice of yer ta join us,' laughs the pirate. 'As they says, old Crivens always gets his man.' There is a sudden swishing sound and you receive a sharp blow to the back of your head. Instantly you lose consciousness. Turn to **158**.

## 283

Almost no vegetation grows in the dusty, windswept highlands. Entering a steep gully you are horrified to see that it is lined with stakes on which are human skulls, picked clean by vultures. At the top of the gully you find yourself at the edge of a precipitous gorge, at the bottom of which, one hundred metres below, is a fast-flowing river. The stakes mark out the path to a rope bridge slung across the chasm, which leads directly into the side of a cliff into which has been carved a massive skull with a feathered headdress. In the distance, surrounded by rocky crags, you can also make out a stepped stone building. You know that you have found the Temple of Quezkari! You have no option but to cross the rope bridge. *Test your Luck.* If you are Lucky, turn to **378**. If you are Unlucky, turn to **63**.

**284**

Hearing you, the two smugglers drop the chest and draw cutlasses from their belts. You will have to fight them both at the same time.

|  | SKILL | STAMINA |
|---|---|---|
| First SMUGGLER | 8 | 7 |
| Second SMUGGLER | 7 | 8 |

If you win, turn to **373**.

**285**

The cannibalistic cook disposed of, you manage to collect enough food for 4 meals before you leave the kitchen (note these down in the Provisions box on your *Adventure Sheet*) and sample some of Bladderwrack's broth (restore up to 4 STAMINA points). As there is no other way on, returning to the top of the staircase you decide which door to go through. Will it be:

| The far door? | Turn to **191** |
|---|---|
| The door to the left? | Turn to **127** |
| The door to the right? | Turn to **141** |
| The door marked 'Captain'? | Turn to **97** |

**286**

You brandish the green jade statuette before the unearthly creature but nothing happens. Quezkari lashes out at you with a taloned hand (lose 2 STAMINA points). You have no choice now but to retaliate with your sword. Turn to **177**.

### 287

Night has already fallen by the time you start to look for the pirates' hidden base. At least that should make your activities more covert and less conspicuous. If you have reason to go to Mandrake's Lane, now is the time to do so. If not, where will you look first for the pirates: around the docks (turn to **67**), at the ruined lighthouse on the promontory to the south-east of the port (turn to **146**), in the sewers beneath the port (turn to **355**), in the taverns and inns of the city (turn to **150**), at the cemetery outside the city walls (turn to **83**) or in the Temple Quarter (turn to **181**)?

### 288

A bell above the door rings as you enter what looks like nothing more than a quaint, tidy workroom. Framed maps are hung on the walls and a bespectacled Dwarf is poring over a chart at his work-desk. As you enter, he looks up and asks if he can help you. You inquire as to whether he has heard of Bone Island. 'Hmm, I'm not sure. My memory's not what it was, you know,' says the Dwarf with a twinkle in his eye. Do you want to see if you can prompt his memory with a couple of Gold Pieces (turn to **156**) or will you leave the cartographer's (turn to **334**)?

### 289

The ship's rats pour past you but do not attack! (Restore 1 LUCK point.) As the squeaking fades, you continue along the corridor. You soon reach the top of a staircase that leads down into the hold but before that are two doors. Thick green mist pours from under the door to the right while the one to the left emanates a bone-numbing cold. Will you:

| | |
|---|---|
| Open the left-hand door? | Turn to **353** |
| Open the right-hand door? | Turn to **202** |
| Go down the staircase? | Turn to **26** |

### 290

In a clear, sandy area between the huts rests the largest shell you have ever seen: it is boulder-shaped and at least three metres across. 'This is the shell of a Giant Cowrie, which live in a lagoon to the south,' Zyteea explains, 'and you must lift it.' Putting your arms around the huge mollusc's shell you heave with all your might. Roll four dice. If the total rolled is less than or equal to your STAMINA score, you succeed in your task (turn to **142**). If the total rolled is greater, you fail to lift the shell (turn to **194**).

### 291

With the zombies disposed of, you can now see that the intricate carving on the stone door is quite clearly a puzzle of some sort, which must be linked to the opening mechanism somehow. If you want to solve the puzzle to open the door, turn to **372**. If not, you leave the semicircular chamber and follow the corridor in the opposite direction (turn to **329**).

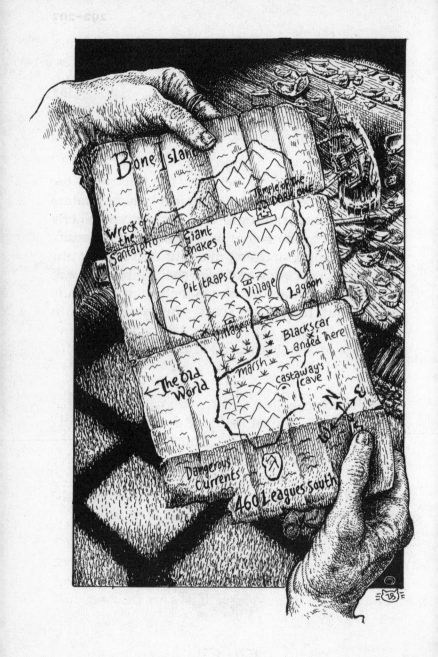

## 292

Finding you more of a challenge than its usual prey, the Scarachna desists from its attack and retreats back into the jungle canopy, leaving you free to continue your trek unhindered. If you were stung at all by the monster you may use one tot of Poison Antidote (if you have some) to restore up to half the STAMINA points you lost in this way.

It is about time you decided exactly where you are going. At present you are travelling in an easterly direction. Consulting your map of Bone Island again, will you continue eastwards (make a note of the number 164 on your *Adventure Sheet* and turn to **192**), head southeast (turn to **397**) or change course totally and go southwards (turn to **68**)?

## 293

Having smashed the bottle, and been cut by a shard of glass (lose 1 STAMINA point), you wait for a minute in case the sound of breaking glass has attracted anyone's attention. No pirates burst into the cabin so you proceed to examine the wreckage of the ship. Inside its fragile hull is a scroll. Unrolling the parchment you see that it is a map of a place called Bone Island (see the illustration opposite this page). Written at the bottom of the map are the words, '460 leagues south'. Taking the map with you, you decide that it is time to leave Cinnabar's cabin. *Test your Luck*. If you are Lucky, turn to **233**. If you are Unlucky, turn to **253**.

## 294

Calabrius's Calculator is a large, mechanical contraption, made up of countless cogs, levers and crankshafts. The main feature of the machine, however, is a large panel with five windows in it, behind which are five drums with numbers embossed on them. Standing next to the calculating device is its operator, a wizardly-looking man who you assume is Calabrius. 'Step up, step up. Who will accept the challenge of Calabrius's Calculator? Only two Gold Pieces and you could win ten!' the man calls out. You imagine that this challenge involves solving some kind of puzzle generated by the machine. If you want to accept Calabrius's challenge (turn to **364**). If not, you can look at the Arrow of Providence (turn to **81**), visit 'The Amazing Armarno' (turn to **9**) or now leave the Gambling Pits (turn to **207**).

## 295

The new tunnel leads you through an archway and into a great cavern. The path you are on curves around the side of an abyss, descending slightly as it does so. Peering over the ledge you can just make out the jagged stalagmites on the bone-littered cavern floor. Bravely, you step onto the path. Instantly you feel it giving way beneath your feet and start to run. Roll two dice, four times. If on any of the rolls you get a double, turn to **272**. If you never roll a double, turn to **363**.

## 296

The sturdy lighthouse door is locked, but using the Skeleton Key, you enter the crumbling tower. Inside you find what was obviously the Wreckers' den. Several empty crates have been arranged around a barrel, which acts as a table, and bedrolls lie in one corner. On the barrel are a candle, two dice, enough Provisions for three meals, and a partially burnt letter. Picking up the charred parchment, you read what you can:

*has been changed. It is no longer 'Leviathan', it is now 'Crossbones'. Destroy this letter at once. Should you encounter the snooper, do what is necessary. We meet at the allotted time at*

The rest of the message no longer exists. This is a valuable clue (regain 1 LUCK point). Taking whatever else you want, you notice a trapdoor in another corner of the room. Do you want to:

| | |
|---|---|
| Open the trapdoor? | Turn to **338** |
| Return to the cliff to explore the cave? | Turn to **391** |
| Leave Mallan's Point? | Turn to **309** |

### 297

It takes two days for the *Fortune* to sail around the perilous Crab Reefs. During this time you are able to rest and recover your strength (restore up to 6 STAMINA points and 1 SKILL point). Eventually, with the reefs behind you, the crew set a course for Bone Island. Turn to **168**.

### 298

'Curse you!' shouts a red-haired woman, leaping into your way. You recognise the fiery woman as Mirel the Red, Cinnabar's second-in-command. It was she who recovered the pirate-lord's body and brought him back to this world. 'Thanks to you I now have this,' she spits, revealing a hook in place of her left hand, 'but I shall make you pay for your crime ten-fold!'

MIREL THE RED      SKILL 11      STAMINA 10

Mirel the Red is a skilled swordswoman. Should you manage to overcome her, turn to **214**.

## 299

You suddenly begin to feel feverish and start shaking. The Mosquito must have been carrying an accelerated, and potentially deadly, strain of malaria. If you have a Poison Antidote, turn to **180**. If not, turn to **367**.

## 300

Tossed about by the waves created by the thrashing Behemoth, you hit your head on a broken spar and everything goes black...

You come to on a sandy beach with the surf lapping around you and the sun beating down on your sodden body. About you has been washed up the wreckage of the *Fortune*. You have no idea for how long or how many leagues you have been carried by the ocean currents, but you feel weary and hungry (reduce your current STAMINA score by half). Fortunately you still have your backpack, with all your possessions, and Provisions, intact. Unsteadily you get to your feet. You are on the western side of an island, and ahead of you is the edge of a jungle. Beyond the trees, in the far distance, you can make out some mountainous terrain and the same to the south. Taking out the map you found on Cinnabar's ship, you compare it to the landscape. As far as you can tell, they are the same – this must be Bone Island! Now you are here, maybe you still have a chance to stop

Cinnabar, but perhaps you should first find out more about your surroundings. Will you:

| | |
|---|---|
| Climb a tree and survey the area? | Turn to **325** |
| Search the wreckage that has been washed ashore? | Turn to **281** |
| Look for other survivors? | Turn to **66** |
| Search for food? | Turn to **242** |
| Set off into the jungle? | Turn to **125** |

### 301

Carved from a single piece of ivory, this charm resembles the head of a noble lion. It originates from a tribe of primitives who believe that it will protect whoever possesses it from the dark powers of voodoo. Return to **42**.

### 302

You reveal the golden talisman to the unearthly spirit and for a moment Quezkari appears to hesitate. Then, with a snake-like hiss, it swoops down at you. You have no choice now but to retaliate with your sword. Turn to **177**.

### 303

The Gambling Pits lie within the area of the city known as the Claws – the poorest and most danger-ous part of the port. The Pits themselves are housed in a vast, stone building with a large, iron-studded oak door. This entrance is flanked by two Troll guards. As you walk past them, and through the door, they give you a cursory glance and one says roughly, 'Remember, no fighting.' Inside, the Gambling Pits lie under a thick cloud of pipe-weed smoke and are packed with the unsavoury and roguish clientele you would expect. Mingling with the crowds, you check out the different games that are on offer. After a brief look round, you discover three that interest you. Which will you investigate further: the Arrow of Providence (turn to **81**), Calabrius's Calculator (turn to **294**), 'The Amazing Armarno' (turn to **9**), or will you leave the Gambling Pits (turn to **207**)?

### 304

The two battling monsters are blocking your way out of the clearing. As they fight, you try to sneak past, without attracting their attention. *Test your Luck*. If you are Lucky, turn to **342**. If you are Unlucky, turn to **386**.

### 305

Your first assumption, that the place is deserted, proves to be correct. Unhindered, you begin to search the rooms more thoroughly. Rummaging through chests and overturning boxes, you find a sword (which will be useful if you have lost yours), enough Provisions for five meals and a total of 10 Gold Pieces. *Test your Luck*. If you are Lucky, turn to **199**. If you are Unlucky, turn to **252**.

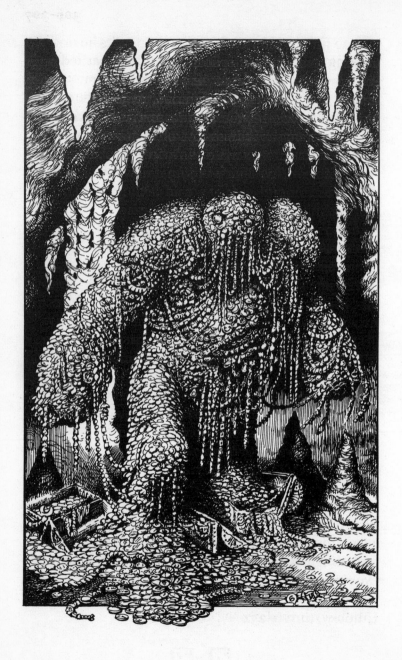

## 306

Picking up the weapon, you see that it has a keenly honed edge and curious lettering etched on one side of its large, curved blade. Hearing a sound like pebbles being tumbled on a beach, you look round and stare wide-eyed in surprise at the sight before you. The treasure pile itself has animated, taking on a humanoid form, and is striding towards you. With the bone sword in your hand you feel particularly adept at hand-to-hand combat (increase your Attack Strength by 1 point for this battle). Encouraged, you prepare to take on the magically created Golem, which watches you with eyes that are pearls.

TREASURE GOLEM          SKILL 9          STAMINA 10

If you win, turn to **251**.

## 307

You draw your sword and lunge at the twittering creature. The Rainforest Sprite hisses at you and jabs past your guard, with its sharp-pointed javelin, which is also coated with venom from Poison Arrow Frogs. (Lose 3 STAMINA points.) Before you can engage the creature in combat it disappears back into the surrounding greenery as suddenly as it first appeared, jabbering away in its own unintelligible language. As well as injuring you, the sprite has also laid a curse upon you. (Lose 1 LUCK point.) Now turn to the paragraph you noted down previously.

### 308

Agilely you throw yourself over the pit and land in a forward roll on the other side. Up on your feet again, you step under another macabrely carved archway into a rough-hewn corridor, which runs both left and right. Which way will you go? Left (turn to 149) or right (turn to 329)?

### 309

The salt sea breeze behind you, you return to the Port of Crabs itself, sneaking back into the city to continue your hunt for the pirates. (Add 1 Hour to the Time Elapsed.) Where will you go now?

| | |
|---|---|
| To the docks? | Turn to 67 |
| To the taverns and inns? | Turn to 150 |
| Into the sewers? | Turn to 355 |
| To the cemetery? | Turn to 83 |
| To the Temple Quarter? | Turn to 181 |

### 310

As you progress through the streets of the port, you feel, with an increasing sense of unease, that you are being followed. Could it be loyal followers of the Black Skull who are on your tail? Rounding a corner, you soon have your answer. Blocking your way is a group of uniformed soldiers led by the Captain of the City Guard. Behind you, several more armed men emerge from darkened alleyways, so that you are surrounded. The stern-faced Captain Snide steps forward and announces, 'I hereby place you under arrest for disturbing the peace.' But this is absurd!

What have you done to antagonise the City Guard? Everything you are doing is to help the people of Ruddlestone and the Port of Crabs. 'Of course,' Snide adds, 'a small payment of say ten Gold Pieces would see you clear of any charges.' It would seem that the government of this city is corrupt to the core! If you want to pay Snide this extortionate amount to go free, and can afford it, turn to **163**; if not, turn to **236**.

**311**

Opening the door you enter a small room with a straw-covered floor, and face the full fury of the beasts imprisoned within. The result of some perverse voodoo ritual, one is a large-fanged, bristle-backed pig, the other a mutated two-headed cockerel. Not distinguishing the difference between you and their incarcerators, the enraged animals attack on sight.

|  | SKILL | STAMINA |
|---|---|---|
| HELLHOG | 7 | 6 |
| DEVILFOWL | 6 | 5 |

If you kill the beasts, you hurry on along the corridor. Turn to **151**.

### 312

You sneak after the men who are totally oblivious of your presence. *Test your Luck*. If you are Lucky, turn to **247**. If you are Unlucky, turn to **284**.

### 313

As you look through the racks of scalpels and other surgical instruments, you discover the partially dissected body of a cat. However, as you reach over the carcass to open a drawer, the cat's head hisses and bites your hand! Lose 2 STAMINA points. In a state of shock you jump back from the table but the cat is lifeless once more. Shaken, you decide to leave the Doctor's quarters. *Test your Luck*. If you are Lucky, turn to **233**. If you are Unlucky, turn to **253**.

### 314

As you search the chamber you find yourself wondering who put all of this junk here and why. Amongst the detritus you find a broken oil-lantern, an old tarpaulin and a splintered piece of balustrade, possibly from a ship's forecastle. In other words, nothing of any value. Now will you:

| Open the flag-draped coffin? | Turn to **36** |
| Return to the other chamber and choose the central arch? | Turn to **392** |
| Go back and choose the right-hand archway? | Turn to **255** |

With the threat of a voodoo cult springing up in the city, you decide you have a valid reason for going right to the top and getting the help of the Overpriest himself. The Overpriest holds court within the most magnificent temple in the city – the Grand Temple of Vinar. Entering the pillared marble hall, leading into the temple, you join the queue of hopeful petitioners who would seek an audience with his Excellency the Primate of the God of Pride. At last it is you who stands before the pulpit, next to the doors leading to the Overpriest's inner sanctum. A pasty-looking priest stares down at you with barely suppressed contempt. 'I'm sorry but his Excellency is otherwise engaged in the Ritual of the Sixth Hour at this time,' says the underling. 'He will not be able to see you now. Come back again tomorrow.' Two armed priests, wearing ceremonial armour, cross their halberds in front of you. You plead with the cleric but nothing will change his mind – not even the mention of voodoo. There is no way you will be granted access to the Overpriest. As you are turning to leave, the priest calls out in a patronising tone, 'Wouldn't you care to make an offering to Vinar?' If you choose to toss some Gold Pieces into the treasury at the foot of the pulpit, make a note of the number of coins and turn to **14**. If not, turn to **209**.

### 316

The chest is not locked and raising the lid, you find it full of fine, and no doubt stolen, clothes and tapestries. Under the luxurious garments you find a large, stoppered Bottle of Rum. (If you want to take the rum, add it to your *Adventure Sheet*: drinking it will restore up to 4 STAMINA points.) Now will you examine the globe (turn to **349**), the desk (turn to **134**) or the ship in a bottle (turn to **29**)? Alternatively, you could leave the Captain's cabin (turn to **233**).

### 317

You grab for the ropes holding the bridge together but your reactions are not quick enough. You fall for several seconds into the yawning gulf of the gorge before plunging into the river below. Unfortunately for you, boulders lie just under the surface of the raging torrent. You crack your head on one and, unconscious, you drown, claimed by the hungry white water. Your adventure is over.

## 318

The pirate unsheathes a long knife with which to defend himself. 'You ain't taken Old Crivens yet,' he spits, vehemently. 'Come any closer and I'll slit yer gizzard!' Ignoring the old man's threats, once again you engage in battle.

CRIVENS                    SKILL 8        STAMINA 7

While you are fighting its master, the the villain's pet monkey does its best to distract you, climbing all over you and biting you. As a result, for the duration of this battle you must reduce your Attack Strength by 1 point and every Attack Round roll one dice: if the number rolled is even you must lose 1 STAMINA point as the monkey has just bitten you. If you are victorious in this battle, turn to 377.

## 319

At your killing stroke the vampire crumbles to dust before your very eyes. There is now nothing to stop you claiming the Scorpion Talisman as your own: it must be worth at least 10 Gold Pieces! (Add this item to your *Adventure Sheet*.) Do you now want to search Jolly Roger's coffin (turn to 225) or would you rather leave this macabre chamber (turn to 166)?

### 320

Coming to the edge of a clearing, you see a tribesman being attacked by the grotesque form of a Giant Praying Mantis. The native is obviously no match for the insect and is in dire need of help – but what have you heard about the islanders? Will you run to the tribesman's defence (turn to **229**) or go on your way without getting involved (turn to the paragraph with the number you noted down earlier)?

### 321

The anchor misses your chest by a hair's breadth. Looking into the fog, you can make out a shadowy figure advancing towards you. Drawing your weapon, you prepare for combat. Turn to **231**.

### 322

You manage to ascend to the cliff-top without coming to any further harm and consider your next course of action. Will you now search the lighthouse, if you haven't already done so (turn to **296**), or leave Mallan's Point (turn to **309**)?

### 323

Carefully, you open the second door. How long has it taken you to get this far? If it has taken 9 Hours or more, turn to **70**. If it has taken 8 Hours or less, turn to **333**.

### 324

By destroying the Crystal of Esoteric Energies you have weakened the High Priest's own magical powers.

Unable to cast his spells at you he pulls a golden dagger with an obsidian blade from his robes with which to attack you.

RAMATU          SKILL 10      STAMINA 9

As you fight, the dagger lets out an ear-piercing shriek, which you find very disconcerting (reduce your Attack Strength by 1 point for the duration of this battle). If you win against the High Priest of Quezkari, turn to **7**.

Shinning up a tall tree growing at the edge of the beach, you look out over a panorama of lush, steaming jungle to the higher ground beyond. From your vantage point you also make out a river running southwest from the mountains to a swamp, and on the eastern side of the island you can see a large lagoon. Feeling a stinging sensation you look down to see a parasitic growth covering the trunk of the tree creeping onto your leg. You must defend yourself against the carnivorous plant.

LEECH VINE         SKILL 6      STAMINA 7

As you are fighting whilst clinging to the branches of a tree, you must reduce your Attack Strength by 1 point during this fight. Also, if you roll a double, you fall out of the tree suffering one dice worth of STAMINA damage, but in doing so you evade the parasite. If you win, or fall out of the tree, return to **300** and choose another option.

### 326

You give the door a mighty kick but all you succeed in doing is rattling the bolts – and attracting the attention of the Wreckers who have been shining their light out to sea to lure ships onto the hull-ripping rocks along this stretch of coast. Wielding knives and cudgels, the Wreckers run at you. Fight them all at the same time.

|  | SKILL | STAMINA |
|---|---|---|
| First WRECKER | 7 | 7 |
| Second WRECKER | 6 | 7 |
| Third WRECKER | 8 | 7 |

If you win, turn to **369**.

### 327

You can now either head southeast towards the lagoon (turn to **10**) or northeast into the mountains (turn to **115**).

### 328

The last of the pirates falls and with some relief you sheathe your sword. It looks as if the pirates have beaten Dregg within an inch of his life and he is failing fast. You do your best to make the old man comfortable and he opens his eyes. 'Thanks, stranger,' he gasps, 'but I'm a goner now. They're up to something you know.' You ask him who he's talking about. 'Cinnabar's crew, the Pirates of the Black Skull.' Looking at the hands of Dregg's assailants, you see that each bears the tattoo of a grinning black skull. 'I've seen them meeting up again around the taverns in the city; Silas Gallows, Keelhaul Jack, old Crivens, even Malu the Witchdoctor. They're planning something all right. Rumour says Mirel the Red found Cinnabar's body and that he's not rightly dead. But he's not rightly alive either, see. It's all that voodoo and black magic they meddle in. Not right so it isn't.' Dregg coughs weakly: 'He's coming back. We'll all be doomed! Stranger, beware the Black Skull. Blood-bones is coming back!' And then he is gone. Laying the old man down, you ponder his last words and what your next action should be. So Cinnabar is not really dead. In that case you may still be revenged. But what did Dregg mean when he said that Cinnabar is not really alive either? Dregg has given you several clues about your enemy and where you should start your search for him. The old man mentioned that the Pirates of the Black Skull were gathering again in the Port of Crabs so they may have a hidden base some-where in the city, but of course at present you have no idea where it may be.

You now have several options open to you. You could visit some of the taverns and inns yourself, in the hope of finding out more (turn to **150**), or you could visit the notorious Gambling Pits, a possible source of information and a way of increasing your Gold Pieces (turn to **303**). Alternatively, it might be a good idea to equip yourself better at the markets before you set out on your quest (turn to **365**), or you could try to find out more about the Black Skull and the cult of Quezkari (turn to **315**). Then again you may do well to get the help of the authorities against Cinnabar (turn to **103**), although Governor Montargo has certainly allowed the port to remain a safe haven for buccaneers and freebooters. Of course you could abandon your search for further information and instead look for the pirates' hidden base (turn to **16**).

**329**

The tunnel winds ever onwards under the mountain. The monotony of the passageway is finally broken when you come to an alcove in the left-hand wall. In the alcove is a bowl of smouldering incense and flower petals. The aromatic smoke billows out into the corridor and as you smell it you begin to feel light-headed. You will have to walk through the smoke to proceed any further but, as you do so, will you breathe in deeply (turn to **39**) or hold your breath (turn to **185**)?

**330**

Baring its blunt yellow teeth and screaming its rage, the Great Ape prepares to defend its territory once again.

GREAT APE        SKILL 8      STAMINA 10

If you win, you continue on your way through the forest. Turn to the paragraph with the number you noted down previously.

## 331

You clear a path to the crystal through the snakes and, swinging your blade in a mighty arc, strike the glowing rock. *Test your Luck*. If you are Lucky, turn to **104**. If you are Unlucky, turn to **376**.

## 332

As you trek through the jungle you come upon a fast-flowing river. To continue on your way you can either attempt to wade across the river (turn to **256**), or try to find another way to cross (turn to **347**).

## 333

You find yourself at the back of a vast hall which is packed with black-robed Devotees and scurvy-looking pirates! Ducking down behind a stack of crates you see that at the other end of the great chamber is a huge, grotesque effigy. The thing has a skeletal human body with an over-sized skull. Around the grinning skull is a feathered-headdress and in each hand is a blazing torch. Surely this statue is a likeness of the cruel voodoo death-god, Quezkari! Standing before the statue is a man you recognise. He still wears the fine gold-braided, scarlet coat of a nobleman and a large tricorn hat but his flesh is now a sickly greenish-grey and pus oozes from great gashes and holes in his skin. The pirate-lord's fine black hair and beard is now a straggly mess and his jaundice-yellow eyes stare wildly from shadowy sockets. Cinnabar! Then the rumours were true: Mirel the Red did find her captain's body. With the help of Quezkari's Devotees, and their dark, forbidden practices, he has been brought back to life. The pirate-lord addresses the throng. 'Pirates of the Black Skull, tonight we sail for Bone Island. There the ritual to complete my resurrection will take place and then, invulnerable, and with the power of Quezkari at our disposal, we shall return to this vermin-hole and exact our revenge. The Port of Crabs will be ours!' A great cheer of approval rises from the amassed followers of Quezkari and your blood runs cold. Although you have no love for the port, should Cinnabar take it over, no lawful city anywhere along the coast will be safe from buccaneers and freebooters. He must be stopped!

Suddenly you feel a strong hand on your shoulder and you spin round to see two ugly rogues standing behind you. You soon find yourself dragged before the undead pirate-lord in front of Quezkari's statue. In seconds he has pronounced his sentence and as you are taken away, he addresses his crew again: 'We sail with the tide at midnight!' Following their captain, the pirates swiftly file out of the shrine. Meanwhile, you are taken to a pit at one end of the chamber and tied by your wrists to metal rings in the wall at the bottom of the pit. The pirates then abandon you to join their fellows. It is then that you notice a small hole in the bottom of the wall, through which water is starting to enter the pit. The hole links the pit with the sea. As the tide rises, so the pit fills with water, and soon you will be totally submerged. The water is already up to your waist. You pull on the rings but they are securely embedded in the wall and the rope shows no sign of breaking either. How are you going to get out of this? If you have a Shark's Teeth Bracelet, turn to the paragraph, which is the same as the number of teeth on the bracelet. If you do not, turn to **132**.

## 334

Choosing a location you haven't already visited, where do you want to go now in your search for information?

| | |
|---|---|
| The taverns and inns of the city? | Turn to **150** |
| The notorious Gambling Pits? | Turn to **303** |
| The markets? | Turn to **365** |
| The Temple Quarter? | Turn to **315** |
| To see Governor Montargo himself? | Turn to **103** |

If you are done with looking for information, or you have some idea where they might be hiding, you could start looking for the pirates' secret base (turn to **51**).

## 335

Passing a rocky outcrop at the edge of a cliff, a strange, reptilian humanoid suddenly leaps at you as if from nowhere. Camouflaged against the boulder by its colour-changing skin, the hunting Chameleonite bounds towards you with its short spear raised.

CHAMELEONITE        SKILL 7        STAMINA 7

If you win, your opponent's body plunges from the cliff edge onto the rocks below. Unhindered, you are able to proceed along the cliff path. Turn to **283**.

### 336

Under the Scarachna's constant onslaught you stumble backwards into its web. Held fast by the sticky strands you can do nothing as the hybrid sinks its fangs into your body, paralysing you and binding you with silk, to be left until it is ready to devour you!

### 337

With you fighting on its side against the Great Ape, the saurus soon overcomes its challenger. Turn to 278.

### 338

Sliding back the bolts you lift the trapdoor and see, cowering in a shallow pit, a frightened, half-starved cat. In fear and anger, it leaps out of the hole, biting you and raking your flesh with its claws (lose 2 STAMINA points), before escaping into the night. The Wreckers must have kept the cat prisoner as part of some cruel torment or wager, no doubt. Now, will you descend the cliff to the cave entrance (turn to 391) or leave the lighthouse and Mallan's Point altogether (turn to 309)?

### 339

The pan hits you squarely in the chest and scalding hot water splashes all over you. Roll one dice and add 1. This is the total number of STAMINA points you lose. If you roll a 6 lose 1 SKILL point as well. A meat cleaver gripped tightly in one podgy hand, the cannibal cook charges at you, his rolls of fat wobbling disgustingly.

## BLADDERWRACK THE COOK     SKILL 8     STAMINA 10

If you defeat the cook, turn to **285**.

### 340

Before your air runs out, you slip the chain from your ankles and swim back to the surface. (Regain 1 LUCK point.) Treading water, you recover your breath and, looking towards the jetty, you see that the Anchor Man has gone, thinking you dead. Back on dry land, you continue your search for secret entrances a while longer but discover nothing, so you give up looking here. Add 1 Hour and turn to **52**.

### 341

The rest of the crew having repelled the other attacking crabs, the *Fortune* sails free of the reef (turn to **168**).

### 342

Incredibly you manage to avoid falling foul of either the ape or the lizard as they snap, slash and hurl themselves at each other. Once on the other side of the clearing, you continue on your way. Turn to the paragraph with the number you noted down previously.

## 343

Having severed the Pitcher's only means of attack you are soon able to finish off the rest of the carnivorous plant, hacking its acid-filled vase open with your sword. (Regain 1 LUCK point.) Among the roots of the Giant Pitcher-Plant you find the remains of its previous meals. However, you also find a total of 7 Gold Pieces, a green jade monkey totem and a rusty cutlass. Taking whichever of these items you wish, you set off into the green depths of the jungle again, a little more warily this time. Turn to the paragraph you noted down previously.

## 344

The Behemoth sucks in a great quantity of seawater along with the wreckage of the *Fortune*, its crew and yourself. You end your adventure drowned inside the stomach of a giant fish.

## 345

Quezkari is in reality a powerful evil spirit, invulnerable to non-magical weapons. Although you valiantly hold off the frenzied creature, ultimately you weaken under its onslaught and join the other souls of Quezkari's victims in eternal damnation.

## 346

You pay your 2 Gold Pieces (deduct them from your *Adventure Sheet*) and step up to the board. You get three spins of the arrow and over those three goes you must score a total of ten or more to win the jackpot. To spin the arrow, roll one dice and add 6: This is the number of spaces round the board that the arrow moves. The next spin starts from this space. You may play the game as many times as you like, as long as you have enough money, but if you win the jackpot, you cannot play again. When you are finished here, turn to **260**.

### 347

It is some time before you find another way to cross the river, via a fallen, vine-clad tree trunk, and your body is beginning to feel the strain of trekking through the jungle. (Lose 1 STAMINA point.) Now return to **192** and roll two dice again, remembering that each encounter may not occur more than once.

### 348

Cross off one meal from your Provisions. The creature snatches the food from you and gobbles it down. Then it cheekily reaches out with its hand again! What will you do now?

Give the creature an item from your
backpack? Turn to **122**
Attack the creature? Turn to **307**
Ignore it and go on your way? Turn to **384**

### 349

It does not take you long to discover that the globe is hollow and opens. Inside is a cloth bag containing 24 Gold Pieces and a diamond necklace. Taking the treasure will you leave the cabin (turn to **233**) or first examine the chest (turn to **316**), the desk (turn to **134**) or the ship in a bottle (turn to **29**)?

### 350

Leaving the Octopus's lair, you manage to ascend to the cliff-top without coming to any further harm and consider your next course of action. Will you now search the lighthouse, if you haven't already done so (turn to **296**), or leave Mallan's Point (turn to **309**)?

### 351

Scouring the various stalls, you soon find a number of items that might be of use to you on your quest. You may buy any of the things on the list, as long as you have enough money (deducting the correct number of Gold Pieces from your *Adventure Sheet*).

| Rope | 1 Gold Piece |
| Extra Provisions | 1 Gold Piece for each meal |
| Cutlass | 8 Gold Pieces |
| Throwing Dagger | 3 Gold Pieces |
| Chainmail Coat | 6 Gold Pieces |
| Flask of Grog | 3 Gold Pieces |
| Poison Antidote | 4 Gold Pieces |
| Gas-Globes | 6 Gold Pieces |

The Cutlass does not carry any bonuses: it is just another weapon. You may use the Throwing Dagger against an opponent before a combat: *Test your Skill*, and if you are successful you may deduct 2 points from your opponent's STAMINA score. If you win the combat you can reclaim the dagger. The Chainmail Coat reduces any opponent's Attack Strength by 1 point, but while you are wearing it, you must add 1 to the dice-roll every time you have to *Test your Skill*. The Grog is very invigorating and will restore up to 4 STAMINA points; also for the duration of the next combat you are involved in after drinking the Grog, you may add 1 point to your Attack Strength – but only for that one battle. The Poison Antidote is effective against toxins and venoms of many kinds and there is enough for three uses. There are three Gas-Globes, which look like small glass spheres filled with a swirling mist. You may use a Gas-Globe before going into battle: the globe simply has to be smashed on the ground in front of an enemy who will then be enveloped by a sense-numbing cloud which has the effect of reducing their Attack Strength by 2 points. However, the Gas-Globes will not affect Undead, Demons or magical creatures. When you have finished here, do you want to look around the Bazaar for more exotic items (turn to **42**) or leave the markets (turn to **111**)?

(turn to **42**) ... (turn to **111**)

## 352

You collapse on the sandy shore, utterly crestfallen. So near and yet so... What was that sound? It was like the blowing of the wind in a ship's sails, but there is not even so much as a breeze. You look up and there, gliding into the lagoon, is a battered, storm-wracked vessel – the *Sea Maiden*. As soon as you are within earshot, the ghostly Captain Velyarde calls to you from the deck: 'Do not worry my friend. Cinnabar has not thwarted us yet. Come, join us.'

In no time at all you are on board: the *Sea Maiden* sets off at once. The ghost ship travels at an incredible rate of knots, flying over the waves as it chases after the *Virago*. During the exhilarating voyage, Velyarde explains his crew's continued presence on the Earthly Plane: 'It was Cinnabar's pirates who slaughtered my crew and I, damning us for all eternity. Now there is a chance to be revenged and restore the cosmic order.' And then in mid-ocean the pirates' galleon comes into view. As you watch, a ball of burning pitch shoots from the *Virago* at the *Sea Maiden*, and it is dead on target. *Test your Luck*. If you are Lucky, turn to **232**; if you are Unlucky, turn to **128**.

**353**

Opening the door, you step into a freezing cabin. Icicles hang from the beams and your breath turns to mist in the cold air. Then the room's occupant attacks. An ill-defined, misty human form springs at you from the cabin and tries to grab you with its frozen hands. You draw your sword and defend yourself as the wraith-like creature moans, 'Cooold! So cooold!'

CHILLER        SKILL 8     STAMINA 7

While you fight the Chiller you must reduce your Attack Strength by 1 point because of the icy cold. Also, for every further 2 rounds the battle lasts you must reduce your Attack Strength by a further point. If you repel the ghost, turn to **389**.

**354**

Watching your footing, you inch into the shadows. The water inside the cave suddenly begins to churn and two slimy, sucker-lined tentacles burst from the sea and reach for you. Quickly drawing your sword, you prepare to defend yourself.

TENTACLES       SKILL 7     STAMINA 4

If the Tentacles score two hits in succession, turn at once to **161**. If you defeat the tentacles without them scoring two successful hits in a row, turn to **280**.

**355**

The port's sewers empty into the open sea through an outlet in the harbour wall. Your lantern lit, you enter the sewer. Following one foul-smelling channel after another, you wander through the labyrinthine sewers, finding no sign of any hidden base or nefarious goings-on. (Add 1 Hour to your total.) Trudging through the cold and damp you slowly become aware of a sloshing sound behind you. Pausing, you turn to face whatever is following you. From out of the shadows emerges an ugly, stooped humanoid creature, with distended arms and carrying a crude club. Seeing you, the Troll becomes excited. 'A Yoo-man! Just what Gunk needs to fill his belly!' Drooling saliva over his tusks, Gunk the Sewer Troll raises his club, ready to smash your skull open.

GUNK                SKILL 8      STAMINA 9

While you are fighting Gunk, you must reduce your Attack Strength by 1 point because of the effect of the nauseating stench of the sewers. If you win, turn to **3**.

### 356

The undead pirate snatches the skeleton artefact from you and snaps it in half before you can stop it. Cross the item off your *Adventure Sheet* and turn to **147**.

### 357

The pirates are not expecting this reaction from you, and you are able to wound one of the rogues before they know what is going on. Fight them both at the same time.

|  | SKILL | STAMINA |
|---|---|---|
| First PIRATE | 6 | 5 |
| Second PIRATE | 6 | 7 |

If you win, the Half-Ogre steps forward to fight you. Will you face your opponent (turn to **187**) or try to escape (turn to **6**)?

### 358

Saying your own name, you try to prompt a response from the primitive. 'Balinac wants food,' grunts the creature. Will you offer Balinac something (turn to **183**), prepare to attack the creature (turn to **95**) or flee into the jungle (turn to **125**)?

### 359

Treading carefully, and keeping an eye open for any more overgrown mosquitoes, you are startled when three figures rise out of the clinging mire in front of you. They may once have been human but the creatures before you now are decomposing travesties, remnants of mud-sodden jerkins and breeches still hanging from their skeletal frames and each clutches a cutlass in its atrophying hands. You are facing only a few of the many who have lost their way and their lives in the swamp. Moaning balefully, the Zombie Pirates lurch at you. Fight them individually.

|                       | SKILL | STAMINA |
|-----------------------|-------|---------|
| First ZOMBIE PIRATE   | 6     | 6       |
| Second ZOMBIE PIRATE  | 5     | 7       |
| Third ZOMBIE PIRATE   | 7     | 6       |

If you defeat the shambling Undead, their bodies sink back into the swamp, leaving you to freely enter the jungle. Make a note of the number 397 and turn to **192**.

### 360

'I won't say any more unless you give old Scrimshaw a present,' the man says, giggling. He will accept any special items or artefacts you may have, including Grog or Rum, but not Provisions or Gold Pieces. If you agree to give Scrimshaw a present, cross it off your *Adventure Sheet* and turn to **41**. If not, or you are unable to, turn to **130**.

### 361

What will you choose? If you want to use a Blue Gem, turn to the paragraph which has the same number as there are sides to the jewel. If not, will you use a Skeleton Artefact (turn to **136**), a Witchdoctor's Wand (turn to **106**), a Monkey Totem (turn to **286**) or a Scorpion Talisman (**302**)? If you cannot or do not want to use any of the above you will have to use your weapon (turn to **177**).

### 362

The few items of furniture that remain inside this cabin are rimed with frost and ice crystals cover the inside of a small, sealed porthole. As you search the room you hear the voice of the wraith-ghost again. 'Leeeeave this plaace!' it screams. You shiver in fear, feeling ice water trickle down your spine and the blood curdle in your veins. (Lose 1 LUCK point and 1 SKILL point.) In terror you flee the haunted cabin. Turn to 4.

## 363

Resounding booms echo around the cavern as the ledge falls away behind you onto the rocks below. And then around a bend you see another archway in the cave wall. With one final spurt of energy you throw yourself through it, into the passageway beyond. Having recovered your breath you choose whether to go right (turn to 57) or left (turn to 91).

## 364

'Ahh, a contestant!' Calabrius exclaims. 'Come forward, don't be shy. Now where's your money?' You hand the man your 2 Gold Pieces (deduct these from your *Adventure Sheet*). Calabrius moves to the side of the huge calculating device and pulls a lever. There is a lot of noisy clanking and the number drums spin round at great speed. Gradually, one by one, they come to a stop behind their windows, the last one revealing itself to be blank so that the panel looks like this:

$$1 \quad 9 \quad 25 \quad 57 \quad -$$

'The Calculator has devised its cunning conundrum. This machine can baffle even the greatest minds in Ruddlestone. Can you work out what the next number in the sequence should be?' Well, can you? If so, turn to the paragraph with the same number as the answer. If you cannot solve the puzzle or the paragraph you turn to makes no sense, meaning you have got the answer wrong, you will have to leave Calabrius's Calculator and look at the Arrow of Providence (turn to 81), visit 'The Amazing Armarno' (turn to 9) or leave the Gambling Pits (turn to 207).

## 365

The port's sprawling markets lie within the Merchant Quarter, which runs from Farthing Lane to Money-lender's Street. You have two possible options now; either you can look for practical equipment around the markets (turn to 351) or you can visit the Port of Crabs' lively Bazaar with its more exotic – and expensive – wares (turn to 42).

## 366

The Witchdoctor's room is full of totems and votive offerings. Amongst his possessions are a Crocodile Amulet, a small whalebone Skeleton Artefact and his wand, which now seems to have lost its power. You may take any of these objects if you want before leaving Malu's den. When you are finished here will you:

| | |
|---|---|
| Open the far door? | Turn to 191 |
| Open the door to the right? | Turn to 141 |
| Open the door marked 'Captain?' | Turn to 97 |
| Descend the staircase? | Turn to 211 |

### 367

Your symptoms rapidly become worse as you quickly succumb to the malaria. An agonizing death awaits, but fortunately for you it will not be long in coming. Your adventure is tragically over.

### 368

The tribesman, who is very eloquent, thanks you profusely for saving his life and gives you a Nauk Fruit (equivalent to 1 meal) before hurrying off into the jungle. (Record the word 'Sitnam' on your *Adventure Sheet* and turn to the paragraph with the number you noted down.)

### 369

The light is snuffed out and the vessel the Wreckers were luring onto the rocks turns away just in time, heading back out towards the open sea. (Record the word 'Enutrof' on your *Adventure Sheet*.) Searching the Wreckers' bodies you find a total of 5 Gold Pieces and a Skeleton Key. As you are considering what to do next, from your vantage point high on the promontory you spot a sizeable cave entrance on the shoreline where the cliff-base meets the sea. Could this be the location of the pirates' hideout? Will you:

| | |
|---|---|
| Climb down the cliff to the cave? | Turn to **391** |
| Return to the lighthouse and investigate it further? | Turn to **296** |
| Leave Mallan's Point? | Turn to **309** |

### 370

*Test your Luck*. If you are Lucky, turn to **341**. If you are Unlucky, turn to **60**.

### 371

Hacking through the jungle with machetes, three pirates emerge from the undergrowth into your path. The first has a neatly trimmed beard and wears a bandana. The second has an ugly scar running from the top of his head down his chest and the last looks like a man-sized monkey! 'It's the snooper!' exclaims Keelhaul Jack, surprised at seeing you still alive. 'Attack!' Between the trees you are able to fight Cinnabar's pirates one at a time.

| | SKILL | STAMINA |
|---|---|---|
| JANGO | 7 | 6 |
| KEELHAUL JACK | 8 | 7 |
| SIMA THE MONKEY MAN | 7 | 7 |

If you win, a search of the pirates' bodies reveals 8 Gold Pieces and a small bottle of rum (drinking this will restore up to 2 STAMINA points). You may also take one of their swords if you have lost yours, then turn to the paragraph with the number you noted down previously.

### 372

Studying the carving you deduce that the inscription around it reveals how to open the door. If you can work out the number hidden in the puzzle, turn to the paragraph with that number. If you are unable to you have no choice but to return to the junction and go the other way (turn to **329**).

## 373

The smugglers dead, you look inside the chest. It is full of counterfeit coins and the villains themselves only possess 4 Gold Pieces. Although you search as well as you can in the mist and darkness, you are unable to discover where the smugglers were headed. There is nothing more you can do here so you leave the cemetery. Add 1 Hour and turn to **52**.

## 374

There is only one dose of this potion but, when drunk, it has the effect of restoring your STAMINA score to its *Initial* level and adding 2 to your Attack Strength for the next battle you have to fight. Return to **42**.

## 375

You dodge the bolt and prepare to attack (turn to **182**).

## 376

The crystal explodes in a blaze of light, blasting shards of rock around the chamber, some of which hit you (roll one dice, add 2 and deduct that number of STAMINA points). If you are still alive, you leave the crystal room. Record the word 'Dehsams' on your *Adventure Sheet* and turn to **329**.

As Crivens' monkey scampers away, you make a quick search of the bodies of your assailants, each of which has the mark of the Black Skull on their right hand. The Devotees carry no possessions but the old pirate is a different case entirely. About his person Crivens has a purse containing 6 Gold Pieces and a very unusual coin indeed. Almost twice the size of a Gold Piece, its face bears the image of a crab – it is a doubloon. Turning it over, you are surprised to discover that the other side has also been stamped with the picture of a crab. Doubloons have not been minted in the Port of Crabs for two centuries and as a consequence are rare and of great value. The coin you hold in your hand however is obviously a counterfeit as it has two heads. From this you can only surmise that someone has been trying to mint their own doubloons, no doubt as a way to raise some money. (Add the Crab Doubloon to your *Adventure Sheet*.) You may also take Crivens' Throwing Dagger if you wish. If you do, you can use it against an opponent before having to fight them: *Test your Skill* and, if you are successful, you may reduce their STAMINA score by 2 points. You may reclaim the dagger after the fight. Dregg told you that Crivens was one of Cinnabar's old crew so they obviously know that you are on to them. You will have to be careful not to attract their attentions further. Hurriedly, if somewhat cautiously, you set off again, away from the markets. If you have the word 'Dnalsi' written on your *Adventure Sheet*, turn to **17**. If you do not, turn to **334**.

## 378

Although the ropes and planks of the bridge creak and groan at your passing, the whole thing holds and you enter the cliff-face through the skull's open mouth. You find yourself in a high-ceilinged, torch-lit tunnel, which cuts its way deep into the mountain. It is not long before the tunnel opens out into a large, square chamber. Hideous painted carvings adorn the walls here but there is nothing else of interest in the room. However, three archways in the opposite wall lead onwards into the temple. Will you proceed through the archway to the left (turn to **216**), through the one in the centre (turn to **392**) or by passing under the archway to the right (turn to **255**)?

## 379

Incredibly you manage to kill the creature in its own watery domain. (Regain 1 LUCK point.) You heave yourself out of the water and take a few minutes to recover your breath. Then, confident that it will now be safe, you explore the cave. However, to your disappointment, no other tunnels lead from it. The pirates' hideout obviously isn't here. Turn to **350**.

## 380

The spider-scorpion strikes you with its sting, injecting its virulent poison directly into your bloodstream. (Lose 6 STAMINA points rather than the usual 2.) If you are still alive, reeling from the effects of the toxin, you continue your battle against the Scarachna. Return to **144**.

## 381

The castaway is happy to have someone to talk to having been alone on the island for so many years. Scrimshaw tells you that he was one of the crew of the notorious Blackscar and was marooned by him once the legendary pirate had hidden his treasure. He also says that the island is home to a warrior-tribe who live in fear of an evil priest. If you want to now ask him more about Blackscar's treasure, turn to **360**, otherwise you can leave the old man and explore the hills alone (turn to **65**).

## 382

Somewhat uncertainly, you hand over the 4 Gold Pieces (deduct them from your *Adventure Sheet*). 'Sit down and rest your weary feet,' says Madame Galbo in a soothing voice, and you comply willingly. 'You seek the followers of Quezkari for you fear they will return their pirate-lord to life?' You nod to confirm the wisewoman's thoughts. 'Your fears are well founded, for I have spoken with the spirits. Even now, those loyal to the Black Skull and Cinnabar make blood offerings to the death-god to restore the Pillager so that he may continue his reign of terror on the twelve seas of Titan. A champion, such as you, must stop them for theirs is the way of voodoo. Voodoo magic is the magic of wild, untamed places. It is the magic of the jungle, primal and savage. It is primitive, bestial and dark. If Cinnabar returns he will be unstoppable and will enslave all of this city to his bloodthirsty master. I can help you in one of three ways for you cannot delay here – time is short. Do you

want me to look into your future to help you (turn to 11), heal your wounds (turn to **179**) or prepare you a compound that may be of use in your trial (turn to **261**)?'

### 383

The tendril manages to wrap itself around you and, before you can do anything to free yourself, it drags you into the vase of the Pitcher Plant. The vase is filled with a potent natural acid, which is how the plant digests its food – and you have just become its next meal. Your adventure comes to an agonising end here.

### 384

The creature does not appreciate being ignored and jabbers away at you in its own unintelligible language, but does not attack, so you set off through the jungle once more. However, as you leave, and unknown to you, the spiteful Rainforest Sprite steals one item and one meal's worth of your Provisions from your backpack as you depart. Cross these things off your *Adventure Sheet* and then turn to the paragraph you noted down previously.

### 385

Chopping your way onwards through the sweltering jungle, you become lulled into a false sense of security. Slowly you are alerted to the presence of something moving in the trees above you. You freeze and look up into the canopy. There, clinging to the branches by its eight legs, is a monstrous, red spider with a scorpion's tail and sting arched over its back.

The spider-scorpion hybrid instantly shoots a sticky silk-like substance from its mouth directly at you. *Test your Skill*. If you are successful, turn to **144**. If you fail, turn to **84**.

## 386

As you try to creep past, the lizard's lashing tail strikes you and the ape accidentally lands a crushing blow against your shoulder. Lose 4 STAMINA points. Once on the other side of the clearing, you continue on your way. Turn to the paragraph with the number you noted down previously.

## 387

Some of the wreckage from Conyn's ship is still half-submerged in the sea. As you scour the flotsam and jetsam you reach under the broken hull of a jolly boat and are bitten by an eel hiding there (lose 2 STAMINA points). The rest of your search proves fruitless, so you give up on this course of action. Return to **300** and choose an option you have not picked already.

## 388

On touching the pearl you feel a warm tingling sensation in your arm. Holding the pearl in both hands your whole body is filled with revitalizing energy. Restore both you STAMINA and SKILL scores to their *Initial* levels and regain 2 LUCK points. Blessed by the life-giving pearl which Ramatu stole from the Usai tribe, you can now either take the fetish as well (turn to **210**) or leave the temple (turn to **188**).

### 389

With a fading moan the blood-freezing spirit dissolves into the chilling mist that fills the cabin. Do you want to depart the cabin yourself (turn to 4), or do you want to explore the room first (turn to 362)?

### 390

The bounty hunter finally agrees to approach the vessel but will have nothing to do with the ship himself. As the *Fortune* nears the *Sea Maiden* you see that its sails are rotten and the planks it is constructed from are covered with algae. Only the ghost ship's figurehead of a beautiful young woman appears untarnished. You can see no one on deck, the only sound being the moan of the wind in the ship's sails and the creaking of the mast. Do you want to personally board the *Sea Maiden* to explore it further (turn to 238) or leave the vessel on its eternal voyage (turn to 153)?

### 391

In the darkness, and with the rocks constantly splashed by sea-spray, your descent is somewhat dangerous. *Test your Skill* three times. If you fail any of the rolls, turn to 114. If you pass all of the rolls, turn to 219.

### 392

The tunnel you find yourself in has been cut from the bedrock of the mountain itself. Creeping through the gloom you hear a skittering sound ahead of you. Then three stunted figures appear to coalesce from out of the darkness. At first you think they are pygmies but then you realise that there is something horribly wrong. The pallid grey flesh, the sightless white eyes, the slack dead expressions – these pygmies are already dead and have been brought back to life by some unholy power. And you are going to have to fight them.

|  | SKILL | STAMINA |
|---|---|---|
| First ZOMBIE PYGMY | 6 | 5 |
| Second ZOMBIE PYGMY | 5 | 5 |
| Third ZOMBIE PYGMY | 6 | 4 |

The first and second pygmy attack you at the same time with their stabbing javelins whilst the third attempts to hit you with poison darts from its deadly blowpipe. Every other Attack Round, roll for the third pygmy's Attack Strength as well. If it is greater than yours it manages to hit you with one of its darts, causing you to lose an additional 2 points of STAMINA. Once you have defeated the first and second Zombie Pygmy you may then fight the third as normal. If you survive this encounter, turn to **20**.

#### 393

'Ah yes,' grins the guru, accepting your money happily (cross off the 2 Gold Pieces from your *Adventure Sheet*), 'you are the curse-lifter, the ridder of evil, the seeker of truth, the righter of wrongs.' You have a feeling this is what the wise man tells all his punters. 'Beware, vengeance-seeker, for a watery grave awaits you between the Crab's claws and the under-tunnels hold nothing but death. Search out the beacon and the woman of the taboo path.' Mystified, you ponder what to do next. Will you consult the blind seer (turn to **167**) or the mute fortune-teller (turn to **98**) for another 2 Gold Pieces, or would you rather now leave the Temple Quarter (add 1 Hour and turn to **334**)?

### 394

Trapping the Jaguar in a headlock you beat the cat into submission. Victorious, you are pulled from the pit and have your weapon returned. Turn to **142**.

### 395

At your final blow, your ghostly adversary reels and then rises up again, apparently unharmed and smiling, as are the other undead! 'Thank you, brave warrior,' says the captain in more human tones. 'Years ago we were damned to sail the twilight way by a foul-begotten pirate-lord. By besting me in battle, you have released us from our hellish curse. We shall be eternally grateful but now you must leave our ship, and quickly.' Not waiting for an explanation you rush back to the deck and disembark the *Sea Maiden*. (Add the word 'Nediam' to your *Adventure Sheet* and regain 1 LUCK point for lifting the curse.) Turn to **153**.

### 396

Turning a corner you feel a sharp pinprick in the back of your neck. Putting your hand to the place, you pull a tiny dart from your skin. Its tip is stained with a dark liquid – pois... Turn to **158**.

### 397

Dusk is falling as you come to the outskirts of a group of mud huts in a large clearing in the jungle. You can see tribespeople going about their business within the village but how do you think they'd react to a stranger not native to Bone Island? Will you enter the village (turn to **274**) or give it a wide berth and camp for the night in the jungle (turn to **164**)?

### 398

Could it be? Hastily you pull the tiny grimacing idol from your backpack and know that you are correct in your assumptions by Cinnabar's reaction: his heart is actually enclosed inside the fetish of the voodoo death-god! 'What are you doing with that?' the pirate-lord gasps in horror. 'Look, I'll give you anything you desire; gold, jewels, why even the Port of Crabs if you so wish. Only spare me!' Cinnabar has shown himself to be the pitiful coward he really is. The only thing he owes you for the slaughter of your family is his death! Hurling the fetish onto the deck you smash it open and pierce Cinnabar's heart with the tip of your sword. With a spine-chilling wail, Cinnabar collapses in front of you. Immediately his flesh starts to decay, dissolving into a grey-green sludge as it drops from his bones, which in turn crumble to dust. Soon all that is left of the foul pirate-lord are his clothes. The butcher known as Bloodbones is truly dead at last (regain 1 LUCK point).

Suddenly a cloud of thick, black smoke starts to pour from the shattered pieces of the broken fetish. The vapour coalesces and then solidifies before you into a terrifying form: the true source of Cinnabar's power is manifesting itself. Standing where the pirate fell is a grotesque creature with a withered, skeletal human body and a grossly over-large skull-like head, adorned with a feathered headdress. At the death of his servant, Quezkari himself has come to seek your demise! Will you try to use something against the horror (turn to **361**) or attack it with your weapon (turn to **177**)?

### 399
The Darkwood Armband is carved to look like a snake with its tail in its mouth. Putting it on does not make you feel any different – at least not at the moment. Now return to **42**.

### 400
At your killing blow, Quezkari's rapidly decomposing body is engulfed in flames. Looking about you, you see that, having lost their leader and witnessed the defeat of their 'god', the pirates are running around in disarray and have almost been suppressed by the undead crew of the *Sea Maiden*. Your attention is drawn back to Quezkari's corpse by the raging fire that has now spread to the deck and

mast of the *Virago*. 'Hurry, my friend!' calls Velyarde. 'We are done here.'

Fleeing the pirate vessel with the rest of Velyarde's crew, once you are back on board the ghost ship you watch from a safe distance as the galleon is consumed by flames and then finally sinks beneath the waves. Thanks to you, the cruel pirate-lord Cinnabar has been destroyed, along with his evil master Quezkari, and the Pirates of the Black Skull are no more. Your homeland is safe.

As the sun sinks towards the horizon, tingeing the Western Ocean a brilliant orange, you gaze out across the watery expanse deep in thought. You are stirred from your reverie by Captain Velyarde as he joins you at the prow. 'Before we must depart this world for good, may I pay you one last service for freeing us from our unending torment, by taking you to some port?' he asks.

'Yes,' you say in reply, 'Clam Beach. Take me home.'

# CHOOSE YOUR ADVENTURER

Here at your disposal are three adventurers to choose from. Over the page are the rules for Fighting Fantasy to help you on your way. However, if you wish to begin your adventure immediately, study the characters carefully, log your chosen attributes on the *Adventure Sheet* and you can begin!

## *Kelyn the Corsairn*

After the murder of his family by the fell pirate-lord Cinnabar, Kelyn took to the sea himself, soon falling in with ruffians and ne'er-do-wells. Eventually he was forced to join Captain Barbarossa's crew of buccaneers aboard the *Kraken*, a feared brigantine operating out of the Bird Islands off the southern coast of Analand. However, on the very day he turned eighteen, Kelyn challenged the scurvy knave Barbarossa to a duel from which he emerged victorious. With revenge in his heart, and with the *Kraken* under his command, he set sail for Ruddlestone again, although it would be another four disastrous years before he arrived at the Port of Crabs, losing both ship and crew in the process.

Kelyn is handy with a cutlass and a life at sea has made him strong, but it would seem that he is under some dark curse as he is dogged by ill fortune. But perhaps all that is about to change ...

| Skill | 11 |
|---|---|
| Stamina | 19 |
| Luck | 8 |
| Gold Pieces | 14 |

## *Griffin Teague*

Youngest son of the blacksmith of Clam Beach, his mother the daughter of a fisherman from Lobster Sands, Griffin inherited both his father's strength and his mother's natural charm. He can shoe a horse and temper a blade as well as any metal-worker, but he feels most at home on the open sea, having inherited his grandfather's sea legs. Indeed, some people go so far as to say that it's salt water than runs in his veins, and not blood!

Normally slow to anger and steady in his ways, the mere mention of pirates will have Griffin reaching for his sword as a red mist overcomes him. Few of those who have ever seen him in this state have lived to tell the tale and now that he has tracked his father's killer to his lair only the blood of the infamous Bloodbones can hope to assuage his vengeful rage.

| Skill | 8 |
|---|---|
| Stamina | 21 |
| Luck | 9 |
| Gold Pieces | 18 |

## Bronwyn Ravenblade

Only daughter of the celebrated adventurer Ragnar Ravenblade, according to her grandmother, Bronwyn was born under a lucky star. But Bronwyn didn't think so the day her kinsfolk were butchered by the Pirates of the Black Skull. And yet she survived and grew to adulthood that she might one day be avenged. She was also the only survivor of a storm that claimed three ships in the Onyx Sea. And then there was the time when she was attacked by a Great Eel in a lone fishing smack two days out of Pollua, the huge sea serpent managing to skewer itself on the mast of the boat before Bronwyn had even managed to unsheathe her blade to defend herself.

Cunning and clever, Bronwyn has a taste for the gaming table but fortunately she usually comes away better off than when she started. She has saved much of her winnings so that she might prepare herself thoroughly for the travails that she knows now lie ahead of her.

| Skill | 10 |
|---|---|
| Stamina | 16 |
| Luck | 12 |
| Gold Pieces | 22 |

# RULES AND EQUIPMENT

## INTRODUCTION

Before embarking on your adventure, you must first determine your own strengths and weaknesses. You use dice to determine your initial scores. On pages 226–227 there is an *Adventure Sheet*, which you may use to record the details of your adventure. On it you will find boxes for recording the scores of your attributes. You are advised either to record your scores on the *Adventure Sheet* in pencil or to make photocopies of the sheet for use in future adventures.

### Skill, Stamina and Luck

Roll one dice. Add 6 to the number rolled and enter this total in the SKILL box on the *Adventure Sheet*.

Roll two dice. Add 12 to the number rolled and enter this total in the STAMINA box.

Roll one dice. Add 6 to the number and enter this total in the LUCK box.

For reasons that will be explained below, all your scores will change constantly during the adventure. You must keep an accurate record of these scores, and for this reason you are advised to write small in the boxes or to keep an eraser handy. But never rub out your *Initial* scores. Although you may be awarded additional SKILL, STAMINA and LUCK points, their totals may never exceed their *Initial* scores, except on those very rare occasions when the text specifically tells you so.

Your SKILL reflects your expertise in combat, your dexterity and agility. Your STAMINA score reflects how healthy and physically fit you are. Your LUCK score indicates how lucky you are.

## Battles

During your adventure you will often encounter hostile creatures which will attack you, and you yourself may choose to draw your sword against an enemy you chance across. In some such situations you may be given special options allowing you to deal with the encounter in an unusual manner, but in most cases you will have to resolve battles as described below.

Enter your opponent's SKILL and STAMINA scores in the first vacant Monster Encounter Box found at the back of the book. You should also make a note of any special abilities or instructions, which are unique to that particular opponent. Then follow this sequence:

1. Roll both dice for your opponent. Add its SKILL score to the total rolled, to find its Attack Strength.
2. Roll both dice for yourself, then add your current SKILL score to find your Attack Strength.
3. If your Attack Strength is higher than your opponent's, you have wounded it: proceed to step 4. If your opponent's Attack Strength is higher than yours, it has wounded you: proceed to step 5. If both Attack Strength totals are the same, you have avoided or parried each other's blows: start a new Attack Round from step 1 above.
4. You have wounded your opponent, so subtract 2 points from its STAMINA score. You may use LUCK here to do additional damage (see below).

5. Your opponent has wounded you, so subtract 2 points from your STAMINA score. You may use LUCK to reduce the loss of STAMINA (see below).
6. Begin the next Attack Round, starting again at step 1. This sequence continues until the STAMINA score of either you or your opponent reaches zero, which means death. If your opponent dies, you are free to continue with your adventure. If you die, your adventure ends and you must start all over again by creating a new character.

## Fighting More Than One Opponent

In some situations you may find yourself facing more than one person or creature in combat. Sometimes you will treat them as a single opponent; sometimes you will be able to fight each in turn; and at other times you will have to fight them all at the same time! If they are treated as a single opponent, the combat is resolved normally. When you are instructed to fight your opponents one at a time, the combat is again resolved normally – except that once you defeat an enemy, the next steps forward to fight you! When you find yourself under attack from more than one opponent at the same time, each adversary will make a separate attack on you in the course of each Attack Round, but you can choose which one to fight. Attack your chosen target as in a normal battle. Against any additional opponents you throw for your Attack Strength in the normal way; if your Attack Strength is greater than your opponent's, in this instance you will not inflict any damage; you can regard it as if you have parried an incoming blow. If your Attack Strength is lower than your adversary's, however, you will be wounded in the normal way. Of course, you will have to settle the outcome against each additional adversary separately.

## Luck

At various times during your adventure, either in battles or when you come across other situations in which you could be either Lucky or Unlucky (details of these are given in the relevant paragraphs), you may use LUCK to make the outcome more favourable to you. But beware! Using LUCK is a risky business and, if you are Unlucky, the results could be disastrous.

The procedure for *Testing your Luck* works as follows: roll two dice. If the number rolled is equal to or less than your current LUCK score, you have been Lucky and the outcome will be in your favour. If the number rolled is higher than your current LUCK score, you have been Unlucky and will be penalized.

Each time you *Test your Luck*, you must subtract 1 point from your current LUCK score. Thus you will soon realize that, the more you rely on your LUCK, the more risky this procedure will become.

### Using Luck in Battles
In certain paragraphs you will be told to *Test your Luck*, and you will then find out the consequences of being Lucky or Unlucky. However, in battles, you always have the option of using your LUCK, either to inflict more serious damage on an opponent you have just wounded, or to minimize the effects of a wound you have just received.

If you have just wounded an opponent, you may *Test your Luck* as described above. If you are Lucky you have inflicted a severe wound; deduct an extra 2 points from your opponent's STAMINA score. If you are Unlucky, however, your blow only scratches your opponent; and you deduct only 1 point from your opponent's STAMINA (i.e., instead of scoring the normal 2 points of damage, you now score only 1).

Whenever you yourself are wounded in combat, you may *Test your Luck* to try to minimize the wound. If you are Lucky, your opponent's blow only grazes you; deduct only 1 point from your STAMINA. If you are Unlucky, your wound is a serious one and you must deduct 1 extra STAMINA point (i.e., deduct a total of 3 points from your own STAMINA).

Remember: you must subtract 1 point from your LUCK score each time you *Test your Luck*.

## More About Your Attributes

### Skill

Your SKILL score will not change much during the course of your adventure. Occasionally, a paragraph may give instructions to increase or decrease your SKILL score, but it may not exceed its *Initial* value unless you are specifically instructed to the contrary.

At various times during your adventure, you will be told to *Test your Skill*. The procedure for this is exactly the same as that for *Testing your Luck*: roll two dice. If the number rolled is equal to or less than your current SKILL score, you have succeeded in your test and the result will go in your favour. If the number rolled is higher than your current SKILL score, you will have failed the test and will have to suffer the consequences. However, unlike *Testing your Luck*, do not subtract 1 point from your SKILL each time you *Test your Skill*.

## Stamina

Your STAMINA score will change a lot during your adventure. It will drop as a result of wounds gained through combat, or by falling foul of traps and pitfalls, and it will also drop after you perform any particularly arduous task. If your STAMINA score ever falls to zero, you have been killed and should stop reading the book immediately. Brave adventurers who wish to pursue their quest must roll up a new character and start all over again.

You can restore lost STAMINA by eating meals or Provisions. You start the game without any Provisions, but during your adventure you will be able to obtain meals. You must keep track of how many meals worth of Provisions you have left by filling in the details in the Provisions box of your *Adventure Sheet*. Each time you eat a meal you may restore up to 4 points of STAMINA, but you must remember to deduct 1 meal from your Provisions box. You may stop and eat Provisions at any time except when you are engaged in a battle.

## Luck

Additions to your LUCK score may be awarded in the adventure when you have been particularly lucky or created your own luck by some action. Details are given, where appropriate, in the paragraphs of the

GOLD

# MONSTER ENCOUNTER BOXES

During the first part of your ad
important that you keep track o
_ _ _ _ _ _ you will be tolo

HouONS
adventure.
Elapsed box on you
you must keep a carefu
apparent as your adventure p

TIME

STAMINA =

in the ND CLUES
sword a

SKILL =
STAMINA =

SKILL =
STAMINA =

STEVE JACKSON & IAN LIVINGSTONE

# FIGHTING FANTASY

## NIGHT OF THE NECROMANCER

YOU ARE THE HERO!

# THE NIGHT OF THE NECROMANCER

**Cruelly ambushed and murdered.
An evil darker than anything you can imagine.
Can you make it through the Lands of the Dead?**

You are the lord of Valsinore Castle on the northern coast of Ruddlestone. You have been away from your lands for three years, fighting the forces of darkness in the accursed land of Bathoria. Now you are making your way home on horseback, galloping past ancient burial mounds and druidic stone circles in the gathering twilight. Ahead you can see Valsinore silhouetted by the sinking sun. You are nearly home.

Three armed men burst from their hiding places among the stones and come at you. Your steed whinnies and rears up on its hind legs in surprise. Exhausted after your long ride, you are thrown from the saddle. Your horse panics and gallops away as your attackers bear down on you, weapons raised.

You scramble to your feet, your enchanted sword, Nightslayer, already in hand. As the men close in on you, you notice the fourth member of their band for the first time as he appears to coalesce from out of the gathering darkness. He is dressed from head to toe in long black robes, his face hidden behind a grotesque skull-mask. In one hand he is holding a glowing sphere of amethyst that seems to swirl with gathering storm clouds. You have encountered his kind before in Bathoria. He is an acolyte of the priesthood of Death himself.

The would-be assassins are no match for your knightly skills and you have soon dealt all of them flesh wounds. In a few moments the battle will be over. But before you can finish the fight, the death-masked cultist casts his spell.

A ball of crackling black light explodes from the acolyte's crystal, forms into a spear of energy that flashes past the beleaguered murderers and hits you full in the chest. You experience a moment of intense pain like you have never known before as the spell hurls you back onto the road again. And then the pain is gone leaving you feeling numb and cold.

You waste no time in getting to your feet, but to your surprise your assailants suddenly stagger away from you, expressions of abject fear on their faces. Only the Death Acolyte remains unperturbed. Curious to know what it is that has the thugs so shaken, you glance around. On the ground, bathed in an eerie luminescence is your own dead body!

Standing over your dead body, you are a glowing ethereal copy of yourself. Your ghostly form is dressed in the same apparel as your corpse and you are even wielding a phantasmal duplicate of your sword, Nightslayer.

Turn to paragraph 1.

**1**

As you stalk towards the murderous thugs one of the men gives voice to a terrified scream, his face draining of all colour, turns tail and flees. Another drops his weapon in shock, while the third lets out a whimper of fear and collapses to his knees, sobbing like a baby. Only the Death Acolyte appears to be holding things together, his hand moving over his crystal ball, his lips forming the words of some esoteric invocation, no doubt.

These men are responsible for your death and you will have vengeance upon them. But which will you confront first, the three terrified murderers (turn to 2) or the spell-casting Death Acolyte (turn to 3)?

**2**

Screaming like a banshee, you launch yourself at the terrified ruffians, who try to run from before your unearthly wrath. In desperation they fight back but even when one of them manages to get a strike in under your guard the assassin's weapon simply passes straight through your ethereal body as if it were nothing but mist – and you do not feel a thing!

Their weapons may be useless against you but your phantasmal sword cuts them down just as if you were still wielding the genuine article and not a ghostly replica of Nightslayer.

In no time at all, the three murderers lie dead at your feet on the moorland road. Only the Death Acolyte remains. You can hear him now quite clearly, muttering under his breath in some dark tongue. Do you want to strike the acolyte down immediately, without hesitation (turn to 7), or will you press him for information as to who it was that wanted you dead (turn to 4)?

### 3

As the three murderers flee in fear, you turn on the individual who actually dealt the killing blow against you. If you want to strike the acolyte down immediately, without showing him any mercy after what he did to you, turn to 7. If you want to demand some answers from him in an attempt to discover who it was that ordered your death turn to 5.

### 4

'Who did this?' you shout. Your voice does not sound quite like your own; it has gained an echoing, ethereal quality. 'Who commanded that I be struck down on the highway, when I was so close to the end of my epic journey?'

The skull-masked acolyte does not answer you but continues to wave his hand over his crystal ball and then utters the words, 'Begone, spirit! In the name of the Finisher, I banish you from this place to dwell in the Realm of the Damned forevermore!'

It suddenly feels as if a powerful gale is blowing over the moors although you can see no sign of it rippling the grass or tugging at the robes of the Death Acolyte. And then it feels as though you are in danger of being carried away, sucked up by this whirling ethereal maelstrom, and you can hear screaming ghostly voices on the wind.

Roll two dice. If the total is less than or equal to your WILL score, turn to **7**. If the total is greater than your WILL score, turn to **8**.

### 5

'Who commanded that I be struck down on the high-way, so close to home?' you demand, your voice sounding not quite like your own, having gained an echoing, ethereal quality. 'Who was it that ordered my murder?'

The skull-masked acolyte does not answer you but continues to wave his hand over his crystal ball and then utters the words, 'Begone, spirit! In the name of the Finisher, I banish you from this place to dwell in the Realm of the Damned forevermore!'

It suddenly feels as if a powerful gale is blowing over the moors although you can see no sign of it rippling the grass or tugging at the robes of the Death Acolyte. And then it feels as though you are in danger of being carried away, sucked up by this whirling ethereal maelstrom, and you can hear screaming ghostly voices on the wind.

Roll two dice and then subtract 3 from the total. If the total is now less than or equal to your WILL score, turn to 7; if it is greater than your WILL score, turn to 8.

### 6

And then you are no longer upon the Earthly Plane and the Dead Winds are carrying you over to the Other Side of the veil that exists between the world of the dead and the world of the living …

Before you lies a barren expanse of grey rock and sand. Above, the sky is as grey as the ground, and full of dark storm clouds in turmoil. Thunder rumbles over distant mountains that rise to jagged black peaks that seem to claw at the storm-wracked sky.

*If you are to proceed any further through the lands
of the dead, you will need to read the full version of*
Night of the Necromancer. *Can you overcome
the lure of the grave and discover who has
killed you this night?*

### 7

Resisting the pull of the Death Acolyte's spell you rush at the black-robed spell-caster, shrieking in fury. A shocked expression enters the man's eyes and he starts to back away from you. But he is not done with his magic yet. Still holding the crystal ball in one hand he begins another conjuration. Not waiting to see what it is he is attempting to cast now you join in battle with the Death Acolyte.

DEATH ACOLYTE        SKILL 7        STAMINA 7

If the acolyte wins an Attack Round, turn to **10** at once. If you reduce the Death Acolyte's STAMINA score to 3 points or fewer, without him wounding you once, turn to **9**.

## 8

The roaring of the unearthly wind surrounds and consumes you. The moorland road begins to fade from before your eyes and you feel as if you are being sucked up by a whirling maelstrom of otherworldly energies. And then you are gone from this world. Turn to **6**.

## 9

As the Death Acolyte starts to succumb to the force of your wrathful vengeance a look of panic enters his eyes. He abruptly quits his spell-casting and instead hurls the crystal ball at your feet. The amethyst sphere explodes with the force of the black energies bound within it. For a moment everything goes black and then the light of the rising moon returns and the world appears once more around you, limned in its monochrome radiance. But of the Death Acolyte there is no sign.

With the murdering magic-user gone, you are still no closer to understanding why you were killed. You return to your body and gaze down upon the cooling corpse. It is a strange feeling to be looking at your own dead body. You know that you will not be able to rest now until you have solved the mystery of your own murder and exacted your revenge against the one who wanted you out of the way. But where will you go first in your search for answers?

You gaze out across the wind-swept promontory towards the distant Valsinore Castle. Ahead of you, directly to the north, lies the village of Sleath, the castle a black shadow now against the horizon behind it. To the north-west lies the tangled expanse of Wraith Wood where, rumour has it, a wisewoman dwells. Perhaps she could help you in your search for answers. To the north-east, the moors peter out at the edge of the sea, where – when you were here last at least – a hermit monk dwelt, down on the seashore. Perhaps he might be able to help you. However, to the east you can see the dark hill of a burial mound and you feel a strange pull to this place that you can-not explain, just as you do in fact to the stone circle known locally as the Nine Maidens where you were attacked.

*Is it a force for good or one for evil that is trying to drag you towards these places? And do the answers you seek lie within them? To find out, read the full version of* Night of the Necromancer. *Remember adventurer, death is not the end …*

Rather than fighting back with an ordinary weapon, the acolyte defends himself by blasting you with more of his dark magic. One of these bolts of black energy hits you and you are consumed by pain. It is as if the acolyte's spell has burned your ethereal form and causes you 2 STAMINA points of damage.

Continue your battle with the Death Acolyte. As soon as you reduce the evil magic-user's STAMINA score to 3 points of fewer, turn to **9** at once. However, if your STAMINA score is reduced to zero, turn to **6** immediately.

## ONLINE

Stay in touch with the Fighting Fantasy community at www.fightingfantasy.com. Sign up today and receive exclusive access to:

- Fresh Adventure Sheets
- Members' forum
- Competitions
- Quizzes and polls
- Exclusive Fighting Fantasy news and updates

You can also send in your own Fighting Fantasy material, the very best of which will make it onto the website.

**www.fightingfantasy.com**

The website where YOU ARE THE HERO!